THE
MIDAS TOUCH

A BALANCED APPROACH TO BIBLICAL PROSPERITY

KENNETH E. HAGIN

THE
MIDAS TOUCH

A BALANCED APPROACH TO BIBLICAL PROSPERITY

KENNETH E. HAGIN

Second Printing 2002

ISBN 0-89276-530-5

In the U.S. write:
Kenneth Hagin Ministries
P.O. Box 50126
Tulsa, OK 74150-0126
1-888-28-FAITH
www.rhema.org

In Canada write:
Kenneth Hagin Ministries
P.O. Box 335, Station D
Etobicoke (Toronto), Ontario
Canada, M9A 4X3

CONTENTS

INTRODUCTION

"He has the Midas touch" is an expression people some-times use when describing an ambitious and seemingly suc-cessful individual. "Everything he touches turns to gold!"

Usually this expression is uttered admiringly, almost enviously, recognizing the skill and good fortune of a person in achieving financial goals and amassing material possessions.

According to Greek mythology, Midas was a king who lived in Phrygia in the eighth century B.C. He was very wealthy and had more gold than anyone in the world. He stored the yellow coins and bars in huge vaults underneath his palace and spent many hours each day handling and counting his treasure.

But no matter how much gold Midas collected and put into his vaults, it was not enough. He always wanted more, and he spent much of his time dreaming about how to obtain still more gold.

According to the legend, one day a being dressed in white appeared to Midas and granted him a wish. The king instantly wished for the "golden touch" — that everything he touched would turn to gold.

The next morning when Midas woke up, he found that his plain linen bedcovers had been transformed into finely spun gold! He gasped with astonishment and jumped out of bed. Then he touched the bedpost, and it turned to gold. "It's true," he cried. "I have the golden touch!"

He rushed through the palace, brushing against walls and furniture along the way, all of which turned to gold at his touch. Out in the garden, he went from bush to bush, touching roses and other flowers, smiling as they turned to gold.

This is the part of the legend most people remember. Many people seem to be fascinated with the idea of being able to create gold — unlimited wealth — at the touch of a finger. Obviously, this is what people are thinking about when they refer to the "Midas touch."

But the Midas myth doesn't end here with everyone living happily ever after.

If You Get What You Want, Will You Want What You Get?

Finally, tiring from the excitement of touching various items and seeing them turn into gold, Midas sat down to read while he waited for breakfast. But the book he picked up immediately turned to gold. Then when he tried to eat a peach, a spoonful of porridge, and a piece of bread, they each turned into hard golden lumps! Even the water in his cup turned to gold.

The king grew alarmed. "If even my food turns to gold, how will I ever eat again?" he worried.

Just then, Midas' daughter, Aurelia, came into the room. She was the only thing he had loved as much as his gold. Aurelia ran to her father, threw her arms around him, and kissed him. Much to Midas' horror, she grew strangely still and turned from a loving, laughing little girl into a golden statue.

The king howled in anguish, overcome by the horror of what was happening before his very eyes. He had gotten what he asked for, but he suddenly realized he didn't want what he was getting.

Fortunately, this is still not the end of the Midas myth. There is yet another part to the story.

Rediscovering True Riches

The being dressed in white suddenly reappeared and asked, "Well, King Midas, are you not the happiest of men?"

"Oh, no," moaned the king, "I am the most miserable of all creatures."

"What? Did I not grant your wish for the golden touch?"

"Yes, but it is a curse to me now," Midas wept. "All that I truly loved is now lost to me."

"Do you mean to say that you would prefer a crust of bread or a cup of water to the gift of the golden touch?" asked the glowing white being.

"Oh, yes!" Midas exclaimed. "I would give up all the gold in the world if only my daughter were restored to me."

According to the myth, the being dressed in white told Midas to go bathe in a certain spring of water that would wash away his golden touch. He was also to bring back some of the water to sprinkle on his daughter and any other objects he wished to change back to their original form.

So the legendary King Midas gladly gave up his golden touch and rejoiced in the restoration of the simple things of life — family, food, and natural beauty. Midas realized that these are the things that have greater value than gold.

The truth is, we do not live in a fairy-tale world. There is no Midas touch or magical formula for material success. But there are opportunities for those who are willing to be diligent and faithful in the work of their mind and hands. And there are biblical principles concerning prosperity and blessing that God honors according to His Word.

Finding Balance Between Extremes

During my more than sixty-five years of ministry, I have often dealt with the issue of prosperity for believers, insistently emphasizing a balanced, scriptural approach. I have observed many teachings and practices that have both helped and hindered the Body of Christ. I have seen some faithful men of God stay the course and move accurately with the truth of the Word and the Spirit, resulting in great blessing for a host of believers. Unfortunately, I have also seen many others become sidetracked by extremism, ultimately shipwrecking their ministries and hurting and disillusioning many people in the process.

It has been my experience that with virtually every biblical subject, there is a main road of truth with a ditch of error on either side of the road. The Church has not always been a very good driver, often having great difficulty staying in the middle of the road. Just about anywhere you go on the Bible pathway, you'll find people off in the ditch on one side of the road or the other.

Throughout the history of the Church, there have been extreme applications of almost every basic truth or doctrine, including issues such as baptism, resurrection, the Trinity, ministry gifts, divine healing, and the walk of faith. The topic of money and prosperity is no exception. There are those in the ditch on one side of the road who teach that Jesus lived in abject poverty, that money is evil, and that biblical prosperity has nothing at all to do with material things. And in the other ditch, there are people who are preaching that getting rich is the main focus of faith, that God's main concern is your material well-being, and that money is the true measure of spirituality. Where is the truth? It's found far away from both extremes, on much higher ground.

In this time of affluence and abundance, there is increasing concern among responsible Christian leaders over the alarming increase of confusion, error, and extremism regarding the prosperity message. I feel compelled to speak out to the Church at large about these issues and especially to address the subject of finances and giving. This book is an effort to bring clarity and understanding to those honestly seeking to find the main road of truth concerning biblical prosperity.

I suspect that there are a great many people — Christians and non-Christians alike — who, like the mythical Midas, have discovered that there is no lasting joy in things money can buy and that prosperity without eternal purpose leads to disappointment and dissatisfaction.

I want to share with you the truths I have learned through careful study and application of God's Word and by diligently listening to the voice of the Holy Spirit. I pray the truths in this book will help you gain a balanced, practical, and biblically sound understanding of the subject of prosperity and also help you maintain that balance as you travel the road of God's best.

— Kenneth E. Hagin

CHAPTER ONE

'SEND NOW PROSPERITY'

Save now, I beseech thee, O Lord: O Lord, I beseech thee, send now prosperity.

— Psalm 118:25

I believe in prosperity.

Yes, by that I do mean spiritual well-being and physical health. But I also mean material or financial blessing. When the Apostle John declared, *"Beloved, I wish above all things that thou mayest prosper and be in health, even as thy soul prospereth"* (3 John 2), I believe his intent and meaning was to refer to three distinct areas of life — material, physical, and spiritual. His fervent desire was that we should thrive and flourish, or prosper, in every aspect of our being. This is the proper application of prosperity — balanced, sound, complete, and evenly emphasized.

Some people have argued that the phrase "that thou mayest prosper" does not refer to financial prosperity. They contend the phrase was nothing more than a common greeting, or idiom, of the day that simply meant, "May things go well for you."

The Greek word translated "prosper" or "prospereth" in this text is "euodoo." Euodoo is comprised of the words "hodos," which means *a road*, and "eu," which means *good*. Thus the Greek word euodoo (translated "prosper") literally means a *good road* or a *good journey*. So even if in this instance the word did not mean *specifically* to prosper *financially*, at the very least it meant to have a good and prosperous journey.

I have a hard time understanding how anyone could have a good and prosperous journey if he didn't have adequate provisions for the trip — if he was broke, lacking, and in poverty and want every step of the way.

Besides, this word translated "prosper" is the same Greek word the Apostle Paul used in First Corinthians 16:2 when he directed the believers in Corinth to set aside some *money* each week as God hath *prospered* him. Certainly and without doubt, the word prosper can be and is used in Scripture in reference to financial prosperity.

Poverty Does Not Produce Piety

As I said in the Introduction, the Church seems to have a hard time staying in the middle of the road on just about any Bible subject. When it came to the topic of prosperity, the church people of my day were off in the ditch on one side of the road. They had been taught that poverty produced piety and that God didn't want His people to have anything.

I always heard preachers say, "I don't want any of this world's goods," because they thought there was something wrong with this world's goods.

But Psalm 50 proves why it's not wrong to have this world's goods.

> *For every beast of the forest IS MINE, and the cattle upon a thousand hills. . . . If I were hungry, I would not tell thee: for THE WORLD IS MINE, and the fulness thereof* [that means that everything that's in the world is God's].
>
> — Psalm 50:10,12

Mark those verses in your Bible. Meditate on those verses and confess them.

The Lord showed me these verses because He had to get my thinking straightened out. I thought it was wrong to have anything. I thought a person ought to go through life with the seat of his britches worn out, the top of his hat worn out, and the soles of his shoes worn out, living on Barely-Get-Along Street way down at the end of the block right next to Grumble Alley!

That's the kind of thinking many people in the church world have today. But they're not thinking in line with God's Word.

Sadly, too many Christians (preachers included) remind me of young birds just hatched, sitting in the nest, eyes shut and mouth wide open, waiting for momma to come and feed them. They will swallow whatever is poked into their mouths. Many people in the Church have been religiously brain-washed instead of New Testament-taught. Without knowing what the Bible says, and having limited spiritual discernment, they are tossed by every wind of doctrine.

So in time, even erroneous teachings become traditions not easily changed. They are passed down from one generation to another, and the new generation accepts the error without question because that's "what we've always believed."

Learn To Think in Line With God's Word

You see, a lot of times, our thinking is wrong. It's not in line with the Bible. And if our *thinking* is wrong, then our *believing* is going to be wrong. And if our *believing* is wrong, then our *talking* is going to be wrong.

You've got to get all three of them — your thinking, your believing, and your speaking — synchronized with the Word of God.

God has given us His Word to get our thinking straightened out. In my case, God knew my thinking was wrong because, as I said, in the denomination I'd been brought up in, we were taught that it was wrong to have anything. I began my ministry in this particular denomination, and they were great about praying for the pastor: "Lord, You keep him humble, and we'll keep him poor." And they thought they were doing God a favor!

Then in 1937, I was baptized in the Holy Ghost and spoke with other tongues. I got the "left foot of fellowship" from my denomination and came over among the Pentecostals. They were *doubly* that way about praying for the pastor. In other words, they doubled up on their praying: "Lord, You keep him humble, and we'll keep him poor"!

What Does God's Word Say?

The idea that God wants His children poor, having no material things, is totally unscriptural. The Bible has a great deal to say about money — about receiving it to meet personal needs and giving it to support the work of God and to bless others.

It is significant that many of God's servants throughout the Bible were wealthy. I'm not talking about just being *spiritually* prosperous, either. I mean financially rich! The Bible says, "*And Abram was very rich in cattle, in silver, and in gold*" (Gen. 13:2). That verse doesn't require much interpretation, does it?

First Kings chapter 10 tells of the queen of Sheba coming to visit King Solomon to see if he was as wise and great as she had heard. After testing him, asking many hard questions, she told him, "*Howbeit I believed not the words, until I came, and mine eyes had seen it: and, behold, the half was not told me: thy wisdom and prosperity exceedeth the fame which I heard*" (1 Kings 10:7).

Job was also very wealthy. God's Word says, "*His substance also was seven thousand sheep, and three thousand camels, and five hundred yoke of oxen, and five hundred she asses, and a very great household; so that this man was the greatest of all the men of the east*" (Job 1:3). During the trials and suffering he endured, Job lost his great wealth. But God restored Job's riches! How do I know? The Bible says, "*So the Lord blessed the latter end of Job more than his beginning: for he had fourteen thousand sheep, and six thousand camels, and a thousand yoke of oxen, and a thousand she asses* (Job 42:12).

In Second Chronicles 26:5, we read that as long as King Uzziah sought the Lord, God made him to prosper. It seems clear that God is not against prosperity; otherwise, He would have been violating His own principles when He prospered Uzziah and others.

It is important to realize that God is not against wealth and prosperity. But He is against people being covetous.

Qualifications for Walking in Prosperity

God wants to prosper His children. He is concerned about us and wants us to have good things in life. He said in His Word, "*If ye be willing and obedient, ye shall eat the good of the land*" (Isa. 1:19). But God doesn't want us to put "eating the good of the land" first.

Moses was an example of someone who didn't put material things first. For example, Moses, who was raised by an Egyptian, refused to be called the son of Pharaoh's daughter when he grew up.

> *By faith Moses, when he was come to years, refused to*
> *be called the son of Pharaoh's daughter; Choosing rather*
> *to suffer affliction with the people of God, than to enjoy*
> *the pleasures of sin for a season; Esteeming the reproach*
> *of Christ greater riches than the treasures in Egypt: for*
> *he had respect unto the recompense of the reward.*
>
> — Hebrews 11:24-26

Think about what Moses refused! He was the son of Pharaoh's daughter — and he was in line for the throne! Moses had prestige, honor, and wealth. He had all the things the world had to offer. Yet Moses esteemed the reproach of Christ as greater riches than all the treasures of Egypt. Moses saw a difference between the people of God and the people of the world.

Some people are more interested in making a dollar than they are in serving God. But spiritual things must come first if you are going to be spiritual. You must esteem the things of God — spiritual things — more than earthly things.

One qualification for prospering is to esteem earthly things lightly. You cannot put earthly things above spiritual things and expect to prosper as God desires you to.

No, it's not wrong to have money. It's wrong for *money* to have *you*. It's wrong for money to be your ruler or master or for you to consume finances on your own lusts.

God *wants* you to prosper financially! But your prosperity depends on your putting first things first. There are qualifications involved.

In the Old Testament, God told the Israelites to keep His statutes and walk in His commandments (Deuteronomy 28). God desires the same for us today. To put God's Word first and to walk in the truth is spiritual prosperity.

Under the inspiration of the Holy Spirit, John writes, *"Beloved, I wish above all things that thou mayest prosper and be in health, even as thy soul prospereth"* (3 John 2). In the next two verses, John goes on to say that he had no greater joy than to hear that God's people are indeed walking in the truth of God's Word.

God told the Israelites, "Walk in My statutes and keep My commandments. Do that which is right in My sight, and I'll take sickness away from the midst of you, and the number of your days I will fulfill" (Exod. 15:26; 23:26). That's *physical* prosperity or divine healing and health.

The Lord also talked to the Israelites about their "basket and store" being blessed, their barns being filled, and about them being the head and not the tail (Deut. 28:1-14; Prov. 3:10). That's *material* prosperity. But notice their *physical* and *material* prosperity depended upon their *spiritual* prosperity.

Beloved, I wish above all things that thou mayest PROS-PER and BE IN HEALTH, EVEN AS THY SOUL PROSPERETH.

— 3 John 2

John is talking about financial or material prosperity, physical prosperity, and spiritual prosperity. Notice that material and physical prosperity are dependent upon spiritual prosperity.

Put First Things First

The first Psalm is so beautiful and further confirms that God wants His people to prosper.

Blessed is the man that walketh not in the counsel of the ungodly, nor standeth in the way of sinners, nor sitteth in the seat of the scornful. But his delight is in the law of the Lord; and in his law doth he meditate day and night. And he shall be like a tree planted by the rivers of water, that bringeth forth his fruit in his season; his leaf also shall not wither; and whatsoever he doeth shall PROSPER.

— Psalm 1:1-3

So, you see, God wants us to prosper. However, our need is to evaluate things as they should be evaluated — to esteem earthly things lightly and to put first things first.

Folks could have faith for healing or for anything the Word of God promises — prosperity, a healthy, happy family, long life — if they would just put first things first.

Determine in your heart to put spiritual things first and to esteem earthly things lightly. Put God first, even before your own self. You'll be blessed spiritually, physically, and in every way — you and your family as well.

The Good of the Land

I left my last church in 1949 and went out into what we call field ministry. I went from church to church holding revival meetings. I'd been out there for a year, and I got hold of the verse that said, *"If ye be willing and obedient, ye shall eat the good of the* land" (Isa. 1:19). But, boy, I sure wasn't eating the good of the land!

I had worn my car out. I had to sell it for junk. I had three notes at three different banks, and I got just enough from the sale of the car to pay the interest on the notes, renew them, and buy the kids a few clothes.

I had all of this written down, and I went to the Lord in prayer about my financial situation. I was away from home holding a meeting. I was fasting, and every day I talked to the Lord about my situation.

I said, "Lord, You see that I obeyed You when You told me to leave that church I was pastoring and to go out on the field. I did what You said to do. And You said, 'If you'll be willing and obedient, you'll eat the good of the land.'

"Now, Lord, here's what my church paid me, *plus* they furnished the parsonage — the best parsonage we ever lived in. All the utilities were paid, and probably half of what we ate was paid for because people just constantly brought food to the parsonage for us."

And then I said to the Lord, "They also sent us to every convention we needed to attend. The church paid our way there and back, and a lot of times, they would buy me a new suit and my wife a new dress." They wanted us to go to those conventions looking good because we were representing them.

I showed the Lord the figures I had written down. "But now, Lord," I continued, "here is my gross income for *this* year. This is every penny I received this year." It was $1,200 *less* in actual cash than what I received the previous year.

Besides that, now I had to pay traveling expenses, my own rent, and utilities just from the money I received holding meetings in the field. Besides *that*, I had to pay my own way to the conventions that were necessary for me to attend.

So, you see, all that took a big chunk out of my salary — about half of it.

I added, "Lord, see how much better off I would have been if I had stayed where I was? And they wanted me to stay. The church board said, 'Brother Hagin, if you'll stay with us, we'll just vote you in as pastor indefinitely. Just stay here till Jesus comes.'"

Actually, I would have liked to have done that because we were the most comfortable we had ever been in all of our years of pastoral work.

We were living in the best parsonage. We were getting the most salary we had ever received. The church was doing well. But the Lord said, "Go," so I went.

I said, "Now, Lord, I obeyed You. If You hadn't spoken to me, I was perfectly satisfied from the natural standpoint to stay where I was." (I said from a *natural* standpoint, not from a *spiritual* standpoint, because when we're spiritual, we want to obey God. But the flesh is not always willing.)

I told the Lord, "I obeyed You. But now we're living in a three-room apartment. My children are not adequately housed. They're not adequately clothed. They're not adequately fed. We're *sure* not eating the good of the land."

You Must Be Willing *and* Obedient

I was telling this to the Lord and quoting Isaiah 1:19. And about the third day, the Lord spoke to me in just the same way He talks to other believers — we call it the still, small voice. He said, "The reason you're not eating the good of the land is that you don't *qualify*."

I said, "What do You mean, *I don't qualify*? I obeyed You. That scripture said if you would be willing and obedient . . ."

"That's what it says," the Lord answered. "You qualify on the *obedient* side, but you don't qualify on the *willing* side. So you don't qualify."

I don't mind telling you ahead of time, God's Word is always true! The Bible said, ". . . *yea, let God be true, but every man a liar* . . ." (Rom. 3:4). And if *you're* not eating the good of the land, it may be because you don't qualify.

So the Lord told me, "Yes, you obeyed Me, all right, in leaving that church, but you weren't *willing.*"

Now don't tell me it takes a long time to get willing. I know better! When the Lord said that to me, I got willing in ten seconds! I just made a little adjustment in my spirit. Then I said, "Lord, now I'm ready. I'm ready to eat the good of the land. I'm willing. *I* know I'm willing. *You* know I'm willing. And *the devil* knows I'm willing."

Of course, a part of being willing and obedient is keeping your motives pure. God sees the heart of man, and He knows what attitudes are motivating him (1 Sam. 16:7). If a person's motive is not right, he needs to repent and make the necessary adjustments. God is not going to bless someone whose motives are impure. No, that person has to be willing and obedient and have the right motives.

I got the willing and obedient part settled. And I knew I had the right motive. But on the other hand, if I was going to eat the good of the land, the Lord still had to change my thinking. My thinking had to get straightened out and come in line with what the Word says on the subject of prosperity.

These are some of the reasons why people are not eating the good of the land. And it could simply be because they're not abiding in God's Word — the Book that tells them how to do it!

CHAPTER TWO

OUR AUTHORITY IN THE AREA OF FINANCES

As I continued to wait before the Lord concerning my finances, spending time in the Word with prayer and fasting, He said to me, "Go back to the Book of beginnings."

Now that I was willing and obedient, He was showing me how to get my thinking straightened out. I knew what He was talking about when He said the Book of beginnings — He meant the Book of Genesis.

The Lord went on to tell me that He made the world and the fullness thereof. He created it. He said to me, "Then I created My man, Adam." And the Lord saw that it was not good for man to be alone, so He created Eve.

The Lord said to them, "I give you dominion over all the works of My hands" (Gen. 1:26,28). Over how much? Over *all* the works of His hands!

In the beginning God created the heaven and the earth. . . . And God said, Let us make man in our image, after our likeness: and let them HAVE DOMINION over the fish of the sea, and over the fowl of the air, and over the cattle, and over all the earth, and OVER EVERY CREEPING THING THAT CREEPETH UPON THE EARTH. So God created man in his own image, in the image of God created he him; male and female created he them. And God blessed them, and God said unto them, Be fruitful, and multiply, and replenish the earth, and subdue it: and HAVE DOMINION over the fish of the sea, and over the fowl of the air, and OVER EVERY LIVING THING THAT MOVETH UPON THE EARTH. And God said, Behold, I have given you every herb bearing seed, which is upon the face of all the earth, and every tree, in the which is the fruit of a tree yielding seed; to you it shall be for meat. And to every beast of the earth, and to every fowl of the air, and to every thing that creepeth upon the earth, wherein there is life, I have given every

green herb for meat: and it was so.

— Genesis 1:1,26-30

After the Lord showed me these scriptures in Psalm 50:10-12 and Genesis chapter 1, He said, "There's another scripture that says, *'The silver is mine, and the gold is mine, saith the Lord of hosts'* " (Hag. 2:8). He then said, "They're all Mine, not because they're in My possession, but because I created them.

"But who do you think I created the cattle upon a thousand hills for? Who do you think I created the silver and the gold for?

"Who do you think I created the world and the fullness thereof for? For the devil and *his* crowd? No. I made them for My man, Adam.

"But," the Lord continued, "My people have wrong thinking."

You see, the devil can run a nightclub, and he and his crowd don't mind spending thousands of dollars to put up an electric sign to let everyone know what it is. But if someone puts up a nice sign for the church, there are people who will object to that. The devil's got them hoodwinked.

How come the devil and his crowd have most of the silver and gold since the Lord made it for Adam? Did you ever wonder about that?

The Lord said, "The silver and gold are not all here for the devil and his crowd. I made it all for My man, Adam, but then he committed high treason against Me."

Adam sold out! Adam committed treason. He surrendered it all to Satan.

And the devil, taking him [Jesus] up into an high mountain, shewed unto him ALL THE KINGDOMS OF THE WORLD in a moment of time. And the devil said unto him, All this power [authority] will I give thee, and the glory of them: FOR THAT IS DELIVERED UNTO ME; and to whomsoever I will I give it. If thou therefore wilt worship me, all shall be thine. And Jesus answered and said unto him, Get thee behind me, Satan: for it is written, Thou shalt worship the Lord thy God, and him only shalt thou serve.

— Luke 4:5-8

When the Lord created Adam, Adam was *in one sense* the god of this world because God created the world and the fullness thereof and turned it over to him (Gen. 1:26,28).

But we read in Second Corinthians 4:4 that Satan is the god of this world. Well, Satan wasn't the god of this world to begin with. So how did he *become* the god of this world? *Adam committed treason and sold out to him.* Now Adam didn't have a *moral* right to disobey God and sell out to Satan, but he had a *legal* right to do it.

Notice Luke 4:6 and 7. We know Adam turned his dominion over to Satan because Satan said to Jesus, ". . . *All this power will I give thee, and the glory of them: FOR THAT IS DELIVERED UNTO ME; and to whomsoever I will I give it. If thou therefore wilt worship me, all shall be thine.*"

Some people say, "Well, that wasn't even Satan's to give." But if it wasn't Satan's to give, then it wouldn't have been a temptation to Jesus. And if it wasn't a temptation, then why does the Bible say He was *tempted* (Luke 4:2)?

It's ridiculous to think Jesus wasn't actually tempted by the devil. Although we know that Jesus is Deity, we must also realize that in His humanity, He was tempted (Heb. 4:15). Satan showed Jesus all the kingdoms of the world in a moment of time and said to Him, "All this authority will I give Thee and the glory of it, *for it is delivered unto me.*" Who delivered it to him? *Adam did!*

The Lord told me all this and related it to faith for finances. As I was praying and waiting before Him, He said to me by the Holy Spirit: "The money you need is down there. It isn't up here in Heaven. I don't have any American dollars up here. I'm not going to rain any money down from Heaven because if I did, it would be counterfeit. And I'm not a counterfeiter."

Afterward, I remembered what Jesus said in Luke 6.

Give, and it shall be given unto you; good measure, pressed down, and shaken together, and running over, shall MEN give into your bosom. . . .

— Luke 6:38

You see, when men give unto you, God's behind it, all right, but that verse says, ". . . *shall MEN give into your bosom. . . .*" That's why the Lord said, "The money you need is down there. I'm not going to rain any money down from Heaven. I don't have any money up here. If I did rain money out of Heaven, it would be counterfeit. And I'm not a counterfeiter."

After the Lord showed me this, He said, "Whatever you need, you just claim it."

We Have Been Given Authority in Christ

The reason we have a right to claim our needs met is, Jesus came to the earth and defeated Satan. We're *in* the world but we're not *of* the world (John 15:19), yet we still have to live in this world. So we must use our God-given authority to enforce Satan's defeat and enjoy the blessings of God that we have in Christ, including financial prosperity.

Giving thanks unto the Father, which hath made us meet [or able] *TO BE PARTAKERS OF THE INHERI-TANCE OF THE SAINTS IN LIGHT.*

— Colossians 1:12

That's something that belongs to us in *this* life!

Now notice the next verse. *Here* is the inheritance of the saints in light that the Father gives as a result of Jesus' defeating Satan.

Who [the Father] *HATH DELIVERED US FROM THE POWER OF DARKNESS, and HATH TRANSLATED US INTO THE KINGDOM OF HIS DEAR SON.*

— Colossians 1:13

Notice this scripture says, ". . . HATH *delivered us.* . . ." In other words, Jesus is not *going* to deliver us; He already *has* delivered us.

The rest of that verse says, ". . . *from the POWER of darkness, and hath translated us into the kingdom of his dear Son.*" Notice that word "power" again. There are several different Greek words that are translated "power" in the New Testament. This one in Colossians 1:13 means *authority*.

In other words, God hath delivered us from the *authority* or *dominion* of darkness. Well, what's the authority or dominion of darkness? That's Satan's kingdom. Remember what Jesus said through the Apostle John in First John 5:19: ". . . *the whole world lieth* in *wickedness.*" He's talking about spiritual darkness and spiritual death.

We're *in* the world, all right. But we're not *of* the world. The whole world lieth in darkness, but God hath delivered us from the power of darkness, and hath translated us into the Kingdom of His dear Son (Col. 1:13)! That's our inheritance!

Now let's look at Colossians chapter 2.

And you, being dead in your sins and the uncircumcision of your flesh, hath he quickened [or made alive] *together with him* [Christ], *having forgiven you all trespasses; Blotting out the handwriting of ordinances that was against us, which was contrary to us, and took it out of the way, nailing it to his cross; And having spoiled* [put to nought or reduced to nothing] *principalities and powers* [the evil forces of the enemy], *he made a shew of them openly, triumphing over them in it.*

— Colossians 2:13-15

Hallelujah! We are the triumphant ones because of what Jesus did. He didn't do it for Himself; He didn't need it. What Jesus did, He did for *me*. He did it for *you*. He did it for *us*! He became our Substitute. He took our place. And when He defeated the enemy, praise God, it was written down to our credit that *we* defeated the enemy in Him. Therefore, we have the authority to tell Satan to take his hands off what belongs to us — including our finances.

Yet some folk are going around talking about the "warring" Church. They don't know that Jesus has already whipped Satan!

"Yes," someone said, "but don't you know Paul told Timothy to be a good soldier [2 Tim. 2:3]? Therefore, we're soldiers, and we're in the army."

Yes, but it's an *occupation* army! In other words, we just come in "mopping up" behind what Jesus has already won! Hallelujah! It's a *triumphant* Church, not a *warring* Church!

You see, Jesus made a show of principalities and powers openly. That is, He made a show of them before three worlds — Heaven, earth, and hell — *triumphing* over these powers through the Cross (Col. 2:15)!

The Word declares we are more than conquerors and that we have overcome the world through Jesus Christ. The Word declares that we are redeemed from the curse of the Law — from poverty, sickness, and spiritual death.

The Word also says we have been given authority over the devil in Jesus' Name and that we can use that authority and claim our financial needs met. So learn to think and speak in line with what the Word says. You can have what the Word says you can have, and you are who the Word says you are. You are born of God!

YE ARE OF GOD, little children, and have overcome them: because greater is he that is in you, than he that is in the world.

— 1 John 4:4

Now in the Old Testament, there are long pages of genealogy — and it was necessary for the Israelites to have their genealogy recorded. There were pages and pages of "So-and-so begat So-and-so" (all those names you can hardly pronounce!).

After a while, you can get tired of reading all those names, and you just want to skip over them and start reading something else!

But in the New Testament, we can write our genealogy in four little words: "I am of God." Hallelujah! If you have been born again, say this out loud: "I am of God!" (1 John 4:4).

Look in First John again in the third chapter.

Behold, what manner of love the Father hath bestowed upon us, that we should be called the SONS OF GOD: therefore the world knoweth us not, because it knew him not.

— 1 John 3:1

That's who we are! We know *exactly* who we are. According to the Word, we are "of God"! We are sons of God. We are new creatures in Christ Jesus. His Spirit bears witness with our spirit that we are the children of God (Rom. 8:16).

Praise God, "*Ye are of God, little children . . .*" (1 John 4:4). *That's* our genealogy!

Those Born of God Are Overcomers!

Now look at that next statement in First John 4:4: "*. . . and have overcome* them. . . ." Overcome who? All those demons and evil spirits that John talked about in verses 1 through 3. He said, "You've overcome them."

"Well," someone asked, "if I've overcome them, how come I'm having so many problems with them?" Because you don't *know* you overcame them! And because you don't know it, you don't act on it!

Notice it didn't say you were *going* to overcome them. This verse clearly says, that we *have* overcome them. That's past tense: ". . . [ye] HAVE *overcome them* . . ." (1 John 4:4). How can that be? Because of the rest of that verse: You've overcome them because greater is He that's in you than he that's in the world!

Ye are of God, little children, and have overcome them:
BECAUSE GREATER IS HE THAT IS IN YOU,
THAN HE THAT IS IN THE WORLD.

— 1 John 4:4

Paul wrote to the Church at Colossae and said it's "... *Christ*
in you, the hope of glory" (Col. 1:27).

To whom God would make known what is the RICHES
OF THE GLORY OF THIS MYSTERY among the
Gentiles; which is Christ IN you, the hope of glory.

— Colossians 1:27

This is the mystery: Through the Holy Ghost, Christ
indwells us, and we are the Body of Christ. He is the Head,
and we are the Body.

Now, can your head have one experience and your body
another experience? No, it's impossible. In the same way,
the Lord Jesus' victory is *our* victory. When He overcame
demons and evil spirits and put them to nought, that's all
marked down to our credit. Notice it says, "YE . . . *have over-*
come them . . ." (1 John 4:4).

Then why do people have so much trouble with evil spirits?
Because of their wrong thinking! They don't know that in
Christ, they've overcome demons and evil spirits. And because
they don't know it, they don't act on it. But believers do have

authority over Satan. They just need to believe and exercise that authority in every area of their lives, including the area of finances.

Jesus Defeated the Works of the Devil — Including Poverty and Lack

There's another passage of Scripture that would help us in our thinking along this line.

And my speech and my preaching was not with enticing words of man's wisdom, but in demonstration of the Spirit and of power: That your faith should not stand in the wisdom of men, but in the power of God. Howbeit we speak wisdom among them that are perfect [mature]: yet not the wisdom of this world, nor of the princes of this world, THAT COME TO NOUGHT.

— 1 Corinthians 2:4-6

Remember what we read in Colossians 2:15: "*And having spoiled principalities and powers, he made a shew of them openly, triumphing over them in it.*"

Jesus spoiled principalities and powers! If you look in the margin of a good reference Bible, it will tell you, "He put to *nought* principalities and powers." He reduced them to nothing. In other words, He reduced them to nothing as far as their being able to dominate us. Therefore, they can't dominate us financially, either.

Since these principalities and powers are dethroned, why then are they still ruling in the world? *Because the world doesn't know that they're dethroned.* They don't know about it, and, therefore, they can't act upon it!

That's the reason Jesus said He was anointed by the Spirit (and so are we) to *preach deliverance!*

Someone asked, "What do you mean, *preach deliverance?*"

Preach to the captives, "You're delivered! Jesus delivered you! These powers have come to nought! They're dethroned powers!"

Ye are of God, little children, and HAVE OVER-COME THEM: because greater is he that is in you, than he that is in the world.

— 1 John 4:4

"Well, I'm *trying* to overcome them," someone said.

No, you don't *try.* You just accept by faith what Jesus did. What He did, He did for you! Christ's victory is your victory. Glory to God!

Exercising Our Authority

That's why when the Lord told me to claim the money I needed, I understood what He meant. He was telling me to believe and exercise my spiritual authority in the area of finances.

The Lord had said to me, "The money that you need is not up here in Heaven. I don't have any money up here. The money that you need is down there. It's Satan who's keeping it from coming, not Me.

"Satan is going to stay there till Adam's lease runs out." (Then, thank God, Satan is going to be put in the bottomless pit for a little while, and finally cast into the lake of fire.)

The Lord said to me, "Don't pray about money like you have been. Whatever you need, claim it in Jesus' Name. And then you say, 'Satan, take your hands off my money.' And then say, 'Go, ministering spirits, and cause the money to come.'"

This was way back in 1950. And from that day to this, I've not prayed about money. I'm talking about for me individually — personally. Now when it comes to RHEMA Bible Training Center, that's a different thing. We present the needs of the training center to people to help us, because that's not just *my* responsibility.

It's the same way with the local church. It's not just one person's responsibility. We *all* should believe God, not just the pastor.

And yet, right on the other hand, the pastor has a responsibility, too, because he's in authority. He has to do certain things and make certain decisions in the church. And that's a great responsibility.

Angels Are Ministering Spirits

In 1950 when I began to see how faith worked in the area of finances, it was all new to me.

In fact, I said to the Lord, "What do You *mean*? I can understand the part about how we can exercise authority over the enemy, claim the finances we need, and tell Satan, 'Take your hands off my money.' But, what do You mean about the part, 'Go, ministering spirits, and cause the money to come'?"

The Lord said, "Didn't you ever read in My Word where it says that angels are ministering spirits sent to minister *for* those who are heirs of salvation?" (Heb. 1:14).

Because I thought it said "minister *to* us," I had to get my Bible and read it. Isn't it strange how we can read Scripture for years and years, and read right over things and not get what the Word said?

> But to which of the angels said he at any time, Sit on my
> right hand, until I make thine enemies thy footstool? Are
> they not all ministering spirits, sent forth to minister
> FOR them who shall be heirs of salvation?
>
> — Hebrews 1:13,14

Notice verse 13 says, "*But to which of the ANGELS. . . .*" So He's talking about angels. Now look at verse 14: "*Are they not all ministering spirits. . . ?*"

Now notice what it said. *"Are they not ALL* [How many of them? All of them.] *ministering spirits. . . ?"*

They are spirit beings. They are *". . . ministering spirits, sent forth to minister FOR them who shall be HEIRS OF SAL-VATION"* (Heb. 1:14).

Well, that's us! These angels are ministering spirits that are sent forth to minister *for* us. "For" us means they were sent to do something *for* us!

Now over in Satan's kingdom, we could say that Satan is the chief. And, you see, all these demons and other spirits are doing *his* work. You hear folks say sometimes, "Satan influenced me to do that." Well, he might not have been there present at the time, but one of his ambassadors was. These demons and evil spirits influence people. They'll even influence Christians, if Christians will let them.

Well, just as demon spirits influence people, good spirits or ministering spirits can influence people too.

I Put Into Practice What I Received

After the Lord showed me this, I went to the church where I was holding the meeting and stood there on the platform. I'll be honest with you, since this was a new revelation to me, my knees were shaking.

I was trembling, not because I was afraid like someone would be afraid of a rattlesnake or a bad storm. I'm talking about a holy, reverential fear. Remember the Apostle Paul said, *"And I was with you in . . . fear, and in much trembling"* (1 Cor. 2:3). What I experienced was a different thing entirely from tormenting fear. It was a holy fear.

You see, what the Lord had shown me was new to me, and my head was telling me, "That's not going to work." I just stood on the platform, and I said privately, "Well, now, let's see. It takes $150 a week to meet my budget." (That doesn't sound big now, but that was big then.)

I was supposed to be at that church one week. So I said, "In Jesus' Name, I claim $150 this week." And then I said, "Satan, take your hands off my money in Jesus' Name." Then I also said, "Go, ministering spirits, and cause the money to come." That's it — that's all I did.

Later I said to the pastor, "Now, Brother, don't make any special pull for money. When you get ready to take up my offering, just say as little about it as you can. Don't say a lot about it."

'Well," the pastor said to me, "you know our custom. We take up an offering on Tuesday, Friday, and Sunday nights for the evangelist. We're accustomed to taking up pledge offerings.

If I just say, 'This is Brother Hagin's offering' and pass the plate, you won't get more than a dime."

I said, "If I just get a dime, you won't hear me say a word."

I had preached in that same church a year before. This was a different pastor this time, and the only other difference in the church was they had two more church members this year than the year before. The church was about the same size. They hadn't gotten anyone saved.

The last year when I preached at this church, they paid me $57.15 a week for two weeks. That's $114.30 total. And when they gave me that offering, they thought they'd hung the moon!

The pastor who was there then had taken up to thirty or forty minutes for that offering, saying, "Who'll give another dollar? . . ." (Don't misunderstand me. That's all right to do if the Lord leads you to do that. In fact, I have been anointed at times to take up such an offering.)

But now that I'd seen how faith worked for finances, I said to this pastor, "Don't take up any pledge offering."

"Well, uh . . . If that's the way you want it," the pastor said.

"That's the way I want it."

The meeting started and was going well, and the pastor asked me: "Could you stay longer?"

I said, "I've got another meeting coming up, but I was going to take a little time off between meetings to go home."

But in the process of time, he persuaded me to stay on through Wednesday night of the following week, which gave us about a ten-day meeting.

So I changed the amount I had claimed — the amount I needed to meet my budget. Instead of $150, now I was claiming $200. I didn't pray about it. I claimed what I needed in Jesus' Name, and said, "Satan, take your hands off of my finances." Then I said, "Go, ministering spirits; cause the money to come."

At the end of the meeting, the pastor counted up the offerings collected for me, and found that the amount that had come in was $243.15! He was amazed. "That beats anything I've ever seen," he said. "That's the most we've ever collected. And no pull — we just passed the plate!"

Now my experience of moving into prosperity didn't happen overnight. From that time on, I made the same request of each pastor I preached for. The result was the same. With no emphasis or pressure, the amount of my offerings began to increase, and the needs of my family and my ministry were met.

I began putting into practice the revelation the Lord had given me. Anytime you get a revelation from God, don't just run out and preach it. Even though the Lord showed me that revelation in 1950, I didn't start preaching it till four years later in 1954.

Prove All Things

If you get any revelation from God, friends, check it in line with the Word, and then put it into practice for yourself before you start preaching it. If it won't work for you, it won't work for anyone else.

Then not only that, share your revelation with those who are over you and who are more mature in the ministry.

In December 1954, I held a meeting for Brother A. A. Swift in New Jersey, just across the river from New York. He was an Assemblies of God minister and an executive presbyter of the Assemblies of God denomination. He was in his 70s at that time and had served as a missionary in China. He later oversaw a Pentecostal Bible school for nearly seventeen years.

I stayed with Brother Swift in his parsonage and had wonderful times of fellowship with him. Respecting his maturity and experience, I began sharing a little bit of what God had shown me and laid on my heart. After a while, he said, "I see the Lord's been talking to you. I received that revelation in 1911 in China."

Brother Swift got out his notes on the subject of prosperity and gave them to me. They fit perfectly with what I had received from the Lord. Later I wrote a book entitled *Redeemed From the Curse of Poverty, Sickness, and Spiritual Death,* based in part on the excellent study notes he gave me.

When my meeting in Brother Swift's church was over and we were saying good-bye, this respected man of God said to me, "Brother Hagin, preach that message everywhere you go!"

So I began including a message on the subject of prosperity in some of my revival meetings. In some places, the poverty mentality was so strong that my message was not well received. But in some places, people were intrigued and hungry for the exposition of the Word on this subject. There was also great interest among some of the ministers I met.

One pastor listened in rapt attention as I shared what God had revealed to me about how believers could claim the finances they needed based on the Word of God. He was an older gentleman who had devoted his life to the ministry. Most of the time, he and his family had lived in dire poverty, with shabby clothes, a clunker of a car, and a run-down old house.

As I spoke, tears welled up in his eyes and streamed down his face.

"Do you see it, my brother?" I asked.

He slowly shook his head and said wistfully, "Oh, Brother Hagin, I wish I could believe that God wanted me to have anything."

How Much More

I wish he could have believed it too. He was a good man, honest and sincere. Who knows what he might have been able to accomplish for the Kingdom of God if he'd had more resources.

I thought about what Jesus said in the Sermon on the Mount. *"If ye then, being evil, know how to give good gifts unto your children, HOW MUCH MORE shall your Father which is in heaven give good things unto them that ask him?"* (Matt. 7:11).

How many parents want their children to go through life poverty stricken and in want and need? No, parents will work their fingers to the bone to see that their children get a better education, receive special care, and have more than the parents themselves had. They want their offspring to have good things. Jesus said, "Do you think God will do less for His children than an earthly father? No, He will give good things to those who ask Him."

Faith in God and His Word that is acted upon will bring results every time. I could tell you story after story of how the Word worked for me even in the midst of dire circumstances.

Yet there is a man-ward side and a God-ward side to receiving the blessings of God. You remember we read Isaiah 1:19: *"If ye be willing and obedient, ye shall eat the good of the land."*

Before you can effectively exercise your faith for finances or *any* of God's blessings, you must be willing and obedient. Then you must think and believe in line with God's Word and walk in the light of it. When you do, your faith will bring into manifestation what God has provided for you in His great plan of redemption.

CHAPTER THREE

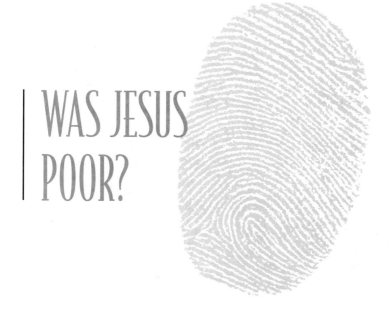

WAS JESUS POOR?

One of the arguments used by those who oppose the idea of material prosperity for Christians is that Jesus was poor during the time He lived on earth. They say He lived an impoverished life from the time He was born in a stable and laid in a manger bed, throughout His ministry when He had no home, until He was crucified and buried in a borrowed tomb.

The idea of Jesus' poverty has been repeated so often and passed down for so long that most people never stop to question it and see if it is scripturally valid. But that does not make it right. In fact, I believe that this commonly accepted teach-ing is totally contrary to the clear teaching of Scripture.

The truth is that in no way did Jesus live a "destitute, inferior, indigent, needy, impoverished, feeble, pitiful, lacking, insufficient" life. Those terms are all used in defining the meaning of the word "poor."

Yes, on the night Jesus was born, Joseph and Mary had to take shelter in a stable. They wrapped Jesus in swaddling clothes and laid Him in a manger. But nowhere in the Gospel accounts does it say they were in the stable because they didn't have enough money to rent a room.

At that particular time, so many people had converged on the little town of Bethlehem for the tax census decreed by the Roman emperor, Caesar Augustus, that there was no room in the inn. In other words, by the time Joseph and Mary arrived, every motel had a *No Vacancy* sign posted. So not having a room in overcrowded Bethlehem was certainly no indication of poverty.

Next, let's look at the two primary scriptures used to sub-stantiate the idea that Jesus was poor.

*And Jesus said unto him, Foxes have holes, and birds of
the air have nests; but the Son of man hath not where to
lay his head.*

— Luke 9:58

*For ye know the grace of our Lord Jesus Christ, that,
though he was rich, yet for your sakes he became poor,
that ye through his poverty might be rich.*

— 2 Corinthians 8:9

The verse in Luke is often interpreted to mean that Jesus lived such an impoverished life that He never owned a home or had a place to stay after He began His earthly ministry. We'll take a closer look at the true meaning of this verse a little later in this chapter.

When Did Jesus Become Poor?

The passage in Second Corinthians undeniably declares that Jesus became poor and experienced poverty. But when? Was it during His entire earthly life? During His years of ministry? Exactly when did Jesus become poor?

I suggest to you that Jesus was *not* a poor man during the thirty-three years of His earthly life, including the three years of His earthly ministry. He was *made poor* upon the Cross when He became our Substitute and paid the penalty and price for our sin.

Isaiah 53, the great substitutionary chapter of the Bible, speaks of how Jesus bore our sins and everything connected to them. Jesus took upon Himself what belonged to us so that we could receive what belongs to Him.

Surely he hath borne our GRIEFS [the word translated "griefs" is the Hebrew word "choli," which means *diseases*], *and carried our SORROWS* [this is the Hebrew word "makob," which means *pains*]: *yet we did esteem him stricken, smitten of God, and afflicted. But he was wounded for our transgressions, he was bruised for our iniquities: the CHASTISEMENT OF OUR PEACE was upon him; and with his stripes we are healed. All we like sheep have gone astray; we have turned every one to his own way; and the Lord hath laid on him the iniquity of us all. . . . Yet it pleased the Lord to bruise him; he hath put him to grief* [*The Amplified Bible* says, "He has put Him to grief and made Him sick"]: *when thou shalt make his soul an offering for sin, he shall see his seed, he shall prolong his days, and the pleasure of the Lord shall prosper in his hand.*

— Isaiah 53:4-6,10

The word translated "peace" in verse 5 is the Hebrew word "shalom," which has the following meanings and connotations: *safe, well, happy, welfare, health, prosperity,* and *rest.* In other words, this passage tells us that God allowed Jesus to bear our sins and sicknesses so that by His stripes, we could have healing, peace, safety, wellness, happiness, rest, and prosperity.

There are other important "substitutionary" verses to consider.

For he [God] hath made him [Jesus] to be SIN for us, who knew no sin; that we might be made the RIGHT-EOUSNESS of God in him.

— 2 Corinthians 5:21

Christ hath redeemed us from the curse of the law, being made A CURSE for us: for it is written, Cursed is every one that hangeth on a tree: that THE BLESSING of Abraham might come on the Gentiles through Jesus Christ; that we might receive the promise of the Spirit through faith.

— Galatians 3:13,14

At Calvary, Christ took on sickness to provide us health. He was made sin so we could be made the righteousness of God. He was made a curse so we could receive the blessing.

Let's look again at Second Corinthians 8:9. *"For ye know the grace of our Lord Jesus Christ, that, though he was rich, yet for your sakes he became POOR, that ye through his POVERTY might be RICH."*

We see that by His sacrifice *on the Cross*, Jesus took our poverty to provide us the riches of His grace. He became poor that we might be rich, which means *abundant provision*!

When did Jesus take on sin, sickness, the curse, and poverty? On the Cross! He did this so we could receive health, righteousness, blessing, and prosperity. He took the punishment that belonged to us so that we could receive the blessings that belong to Him.

The reason I am so certain this is what the Scriptures are saying is because the Gospels, when properly examined and rightly divided, do not portray Jesus as a poverty-stricken individual. On the contrary, Jesus is seen as a Man whose needs were met and who was regularly involved in meeting the needs of others.

Gifts of Treasure

Let's start at the very beginning of Jesus' life. As a very young child, Jesus received some very costly and valuable gifts from the wise men, or magi, who traveled from Persia to find and worship the newborn "King of the Jews" whose star they had seen in the east. The Gospel account makes it clear that the gifts they brought to present to Jesus were not just cheap trinkets.

And when they were come into the house, they saw the young child with Mary his mother, and fell down, and worshipped him: and when they had OPENED THEIR TREASURES, they presented unto him gifts; gold, and frankincense, and myrrh.

— Matthew 2:11

Other translations of the same verse confirm that the wise men brought rich and valuable gifts. The Williams translation refers to their "treasure sacks," and *The Amplified Bible* says "treasure bags." The Modern Language translation says "treasure chests," *The Twentieth Century New Testament* says "treasures," while the Knox translation renders it "store of treasures."

Herod the king, whom the Roman authorities had allowed to be the local Jewish ruler, became very jealous and suspicious of the infant King who possibly one day would dethrone him. So he ordered the slaughter of all the male children in the region of Bethlehem who were two years old or younger.

Being warned by an angel in a dream, Joseph took Mary and the baby Jesus and fled by night, making the long trek into Egypt. So it is possible — even probable — that the "prosperity" of the wise men's gifts assisted Jesus' family in the move to Egypt and perhaps sustained them all the months they were there.

Jesus Had Ministry Partners

When Jesus launched His public ministry, He called twelve disciples to travel with Him. For three years, He and His little band traveled all over Palestine, throughout the region of Galilee, down the Jordan River to the hills of Judaea, and up to Jerusalem.

Even in those days, when travel meant walking or riding an animal, sometimes sleeping under the open skies or seeking shelter in the homes of friends, keeping that many people on the road must have involved considerable expense. Food and clothing for a dozen or more people, day after day, week after week, required that Jesus have enough funds to pay their way.

Where did the money come from? The Bible tells us that Jesus had ministry partners who helped provide His support.

And it came to pass afterward, that he went throughout every city and village, preaching and shewing the glad tidings of the kingdom of God: and the twelve were with him, and certain women, which had been healed of evil spirits and infirmities, Mary called Magdalene, out of whom went seven devils, and Joanna the wife of Chuza Herod's steward, and Susanna, and MANY OTHERS, WHICH MINISTERED UNTO HIM OF THEIR SUBSTANCE.

— Luke 8:1-3

Notice how verse 3 reads in some other translations.

The Wuest version says, ". . . and others, many of them, who were of such a nature that THEY KEPT ON SUPPLYING THEM with food and the other necessities of life out of their possessions." The Williams translation renders the verse, ". . . and many other women, who CONTINUED TO CONTRIBUTE TO THEIR NEEDS out of their personal means." The Phillips translation says, ". . . and many others who USED TO LOOK AFTER HIS [JESUS'] COMFORT from their own resources."

Does this sound like Jesus and His disciples were poor and destitute, a traveling band of beggars who lived off the land, hand-to-mouth? Absolutely not. Their needs were met through the generosity of many partners who faithfully and consistently supported Jesus' ministry financially.

Was Jesus Homeless?

Contrary to traditional thinking, Jesus did have a place of residence. The passage most often cited by people in an attempt to prove that Jesus never owned a home or had a residence is found in Luke chapter 9. Let's read all the related verses in context.

As the time approached for him to be taken up to heaven, Jesus resolutely set out for Jerusalem. And he sent messengers on

ahead, who went into a Samaritan village to get things
ready for him; but the people there did not welcome him,
because he was heading for Jerusalem. When the disciples
James and John saw this, they asked, "Lord, do you want
us to call fire down from heaven to destroy them?" But
Jesus turned and rebuked them, and they went to another
village. As they were walking along the road, a man said to
him, "I will follow you wherever you go." Jesus replied,
"Foxes have holes and birds of the air have nests, but the
Son of Man has no place to lay his head."

— Luke 9:51-58 (NIV)

Reading in context, we learn that in verse 58 Jesus was simply saying, "At this time in My life, I am on the move. I'm going forward on My way to fulfill My mission. I'm not settling down on this earth, but I'm on My way to be taken up to Heaven."

Notice that there are other scriptures that seem to indicate that Jesus did have an earthly home or residence.

When Jesus heard that John had been put in prison, he
returned to Galilee. Leaving Nazareth, he went and lived
in Capernaum, which was by the lake in the area of
Zebulun and Naphtali. . . .

— Matthew 4:12,13 (NIV)

The Williams translation of verse 13 says, "But he left Nazareth and made His home in Capernaum. . . ." Wuest renders the same verse, "And having abandoned Nazareth . . . He established His permanent home in Capernaum. . . ."

Now look at Matthew 9:1. It says, "Jesus stepped into a boat, crossed over and came to his own town" (*NIV*).

Williams translates this verse, "And He got into a boat and crossed to the other side, and went into His home town." The Wuest version says, "And having gone on board the boat, he crossed over and entered his own city."

How does someone have his "own town," his "home town," and his "own city" unless he lives there? And how does he live there unless he has a place to live?

Mark 2:1 is also very interesting. It reads, "A few days later, when Jesus again entered Capernaum, the people heard that he had come home" (*NIV*).

In the Williams version, the verse reads, "After some days He came back to Capernaum, and it was reported that He was at home." Wuest's translation says, "And having again entered Capernaum, after some days He was heard of as being at home."

Jesus couldn't "come home" or be reported as being "at home" if He didn't have a home.

The argument that Jesus didn't have a home cannot be used as proof of the poverty of Jesus because Scripture indicates that Jesus did indeed have a home.

Fishing for Gold

There are other scriptural indications that Jesus didn't live a poverty-stricken life. For example, when it was necessary, God's miracle power operated through Jesus to meet His needs and the material needs of others.

> When they came to Capernaum, the collectors of the half-shekel tax went up to Peter and said, "Does not your teacher pay the tax?" He said, "Yes." And when he came home, Jesus spoke to him first, saying, "What do you think, Simon? From whom do kings of the earth take toll or tribute? From their sons or from others?" And when he said, "From others," Jesus said to him, "Then the sons are free. However, not to give offense to them, go to the sea and cast a hook, and take the first fish that comes up, and when you open its mouth you will find a shekel; take that and give it to them for me and for yourself."
>
> — Matthew 17:24-27 (RSV)

Two other passages in Matthew also illustrate God's miracle-working power to provide for people's material needs. Matthew 14:15-21 tells the story of the feeding of the five thousand men with five loaves and two fish. Matthew 15:32-39 relates the story of the feeding of four thousand men with seven loaves and a few fish.

During His ministry on the earth, time and again Jesus demonstrated that the resources necessary to meet every need were available to Him.

Assisting the Poor

Another reason I believe Jesus was prosperous is that the Bible indicates that Jesus' ministry assisted the poor financially on a regular basis.

The Apostle John's account of the Last Supper is one of the most powerful and moving passages in the New Testament, filled with important and significant events. John chapter 13 tells about Jesus washing the feet of His disciples, foretelling His betrayal, giving the new commandment to love one another, and warning Peter of his imminent denial of the Lord.

But people sometimes overlook three very important verses regarding Judas that emphasize the fact that Jesus' ministry had sufficient means to assist the poor financially — apparently on a regular basis.

When Satan entered into Judas and put it into his heart to betray Jesus, he got up from the supper to go out. John 13 records the story.

. . . Then said Jesus unto him [Judas], *That thou doest, do quickly. Now no man at the table knew for what intent he spake this unto him. For some of them thought, because Judas had the bag, that Jesus had said unto him,* BUY THOSE THINGS THAT WE HAVE NEED OF AGAINST THE FEAST; OR, THAT HE SHOULD GIVE SOMETHING TO THE POOR.

— John 13:27-29

Why would the other disciples have thought Judas was going to buy something or give money to the poor unless that was something he had been sent to do before, or perhaps was in the habit of doing on a regular basis? Obviously, neither of these possible actions seemed unusual or noteworthy to the eleven, probably indicating that they had seen both things occur with some frequency in the past.

Buying provisions for a feast and giving to the poor were apparently ordinary events to the disciples. And a person can't do either of these without having money.

Judas the Treasurer

We know Jesus had *some* money at least, because He had a treasurer who regularly embezzled money from the funds entrusted to his keeping.

John 12:6 says, ". . . *As keeper of the money bag, he* [Judas] *used to help himself to what was put into it*" (*NIV*).

The Williams translation of John 12:6 reads, ". . . as the carrier of the purse for the Twelve he was in the habit of taking what was put into it."

I believe it is reasonable to assume that poor, penniless, destitute people don't have a treasurer or designated person to carry their money around. Jesus and the disciples had enough funds that they put someone in charge of handling them.

Also, the Gospel account suggests there were enough funds in the treasury that Judas could steal some from time to time without it being immediately noticed. A treasurer couldn't regularly embezzle money from the bag unless there was a continual supply of money going into it. If there was enough money in the bag for Judas to embezzle on a regular basis and still have enough to sustain the group, Jesus could not have been poor.

Jesus Distinguished Himself From the Poor

During a visit to the Bethany home of Lazarus, Martha, and Mary, Jesus said to the guests at the supper, "You will always have the poor among you, but you will not always have me" (John 12:8 *NIV*). Notice that Jesus didn't call Himself poor. He made a definite distinction between the poor and Himself.

Some people have mistakenly thought that this state-ment implied that Jesus was saying that helping the poor is unimportant. However, the Old Testament reference He was quoting strongly indicates that this is *not* what Jesus meant. Deuteronomy 15:11 says, *"There will always be poor people in the land. Therefore I command you to be openhanded toward your brothers and toward the poor and needy in your land"* (NIV).

In effect, Jesus was saying, "There will always be poor people who need help, and you should help them as much as you can. But I'm only going to be here a very short time, and this woman [who anointed His feet with expensive ointment] took advantage of a very limited opportunity. You will always have opportunities to help the poor, but I won't be here very much longer."

The point is that not once did Jesus identify Himself as one of the poor. He did not say, "There will always be poor people like *Me*." Instead, He made a definite distinction between the poor and Himself.

Expensive Perfume

We find another scriptural indication that Jesus wasn't poor in the fact that He was not the least bit bothered when perfume worth a year's salary was used to anoint His feet.

Let's examine this story as it is written in Luke's Gospel.

*Six days before the Passover, Jesus arrived at Bethany,
where Lazarus lived, whom Jesus had raised from the
dead. Here a dinner was given in Jesus' honor. Martha
served, while Lazarus was among those reclining at the
table with him. Then Mary took about a pint of pure
nard, an expensive perfume; she poured it on Jesus' feet
and wiped his feet with her hair. And the house was filled
with the fragrance of the perfume. But one of his disciples,
Judas Iscariot, who was later to betray him, objected,
"Why wasn't this perfume sold and the money given to the
poor? IT WAS WORTH A YEAR'S WAGES." He did
not say this because he cared about the poor but because
he was a thief; as keeper of the money bag, he used to help
himself to what was put into it. "Leave her alone," Jesus
replied. "It was intended that she should save this perfume
for the day of my burial. You will always have the poor
among you, but you will not always have me."*

— John 12:1-8 (NIV)

A poor man, not used to having anything, more than
likely would not have had a relaxed attitude to a "year's salary"
being poured over his feet. But Jesus was not intimidated, concerned, or uncomfortable in the slightest about the value of
the perfume Mary used to anoint His feet. How could this be?

Consider Who Jesus Really Was!

Jesus was — and is — the Creator of the universe and of this world! The Gospel of John declares, "*All things were made by him; and without him was not any thing made that was made*" (1:3).

Colossians 1:16 proclaims, "*For by him were all things created, that are in heaven, and that are in earth, visible and invisible, whether they be thrones, or dominions, or principalities, or powers: all things were created by him, and for him.*"

Now consider Jesus' real home, the place He created for Himself and, eventually, for us to dwell in. Remember, everyone endeavors to make his own home a place that is suited to his own tastes, a place where it is comfortable for him to live. Jesus' home was described for us in the Book of Revelation.

> . . . *the Holy City, Jerusalem, coming down out of heaven from God. It shone with the glory of God, and its brilliance was like that of a very precious jewel, like a jasper, clear as crystal. It had a great, high wall with twelve gates. . . . The wall was made of jasper, and the city of pure gold, as pure as glass. The foundations of the city walls were decorated with every kind of precious stone. . . . The twelve gates were twelve pearls, each gate made of a single pearl. The great street of the city was of pure gold, like transparent glass.*
>
> — Revelation 21:10-12,18,19,21 (*NIV*)

Who could design and create such a magnificent dwelling place? Psalm 24:10 gives us the answer: *"Who is this King of glory? The Lord of hosts, he is the King of glory."*

Let's look at some Bible passages that help us catch a glimpse of the majesty and power of God. (And remember, if these things were said of God, they also pertain to Jesus. John 10:30 says, *"I [Jesus] and my Father are one,"* and John 14:9 says, *". . . he that hath seen me hath seen the Father. . . ."*)

Melchizedek referred to God as *". . . the most high God, possessor of heaven and earth."*

— Genesis 14:19

Moses said that *". . . the earth is the Lord's."*

— Exodus 9:29

Joshua said God is "Lord of all the earth."

— Joshua 3:11

King David said, "Yours, O Lord, is the greatness and the power and the glory and the majesty and the splendor, for everything in heaven and earth is yours. Yours, O Lord, is the kingdom; you are exalted as head over all. Wealth and honor come from you; you are the ruler of all things. In your hands are strength and power to exalt and give strength to all."

— 1 Chronicles 29:11,12 (*NIV*)

God, speaking about Himself to Job, said, "Who has a claim against me that I must pay? Everything under heaven belongs to me."

— Job 41:11 (*NIV*)

The Psalmist David declared, *"The earth is the Lord's, and the fulness thereof; the world, and they that dwell therein."*

— Psalm 24:1

David also said, *". . . the earth is full of thy riches."*

— Psalm 104:24

God said of Himself, *"For every beast of the forest is mine, and the cattle upon a thousand hills. I know all the fowls of the mountains: and the wild beasts of the field are mine. If I were hungry, I would not tell thee: for the world is mine, and the fulness thereof."*

— Psalm 50:10-12

God said to Isaiah, *". . . The heaven is my throne, and the earth is my footstool."*

— Isaiah 66:1

Through Haggai, God said, *"The silver is mine, and the gold is mine, saith the Lord of hosts."*

— Haggai 2:8

Zechariah referred to God as the "Lord of the whole earth."

— Zechariah 4:14;6:5

Paul said twice in First Corinthians 10, ". . . *the earth is the Lord's, and the fulness thereof.*"

— 1 Corinthians 10:26,28

Writing in Philippians, Paul said that Jesus, ". . . *being in the form of God, thought it not robbery to be equal with God: But made himself of no reputation, and took upon him the form of a servant, and was made in the likeness of men: And being found in fashion as a man, he humbled himself, and became obedient unto death, even the death of the cross. Wherefore God also hath highly exalted him, and given him a name which is above every name: That at the name of Jesus every knee should bow, of things in heaven, and things in earth, and things under the earth; And that every tongue should confess that Jesus Christ is Lord, to the glory of God the Father.*"

— Philippians 2:6-11

Jesus was with the Father at the dawn of creation and lived in Heaven with the Father and the angels. Revelation 21:21 says that the streets of Heaven are pure gold. Gold to Jesus is what asphalt is to us!

Jesus created this world with all its gold, silver, diamonds, rubies, sapphires, and every kind of natural resource. The cattle upon a thousand hills are His. He created it *all.*

No wonder He wasn't the least bit bothered by a little perfume being poured upon His feet.

Jesus Never Lacked

At the end of Jesus' earthly ministry, His own disciples testified that they never lacked anything.

Then Jesus asked them, "When I sent you without purse, bag or sandals, did you lack anything?"

"Nothing," they answered.

— Luke 22:35 (NIV)

If the disciples testified that they had experienced no lack as they carried out their ministry assignments, we can assume that they had a full supply and abundant provision. At the very least, they had enough — an adequate supply for their needs. And that's not poor!

Jesus Wore Nice Clothes

When Jesus was crucified, His clothes were nice enough that the soldiers divided them among themselves and gambled for His coat.

Then the soldiers, when they had crucified Jesus, took his garments, and made four parts, to every soldier a part; and also his coat: now the coat was without seam, woven from the top throughout. They said therefore among themselves, Let us not rend it, but cast lots for it, whose it shall be: that the scripture might be fulfilled, which saith, They parted my raiment among them, and for my vesture they did cast lots. These things therefore the soldiers did.

— John 19:23,24

Would Roman soldiers cast lots for the tattered and torn rags of a beggar or the shabby, worn clothes of a poor man? No, of course not.

Was Jesus Poor or Prosperous?

Let's go back to our original question. I believe the Bible addresses this issue in detail and offers a clear and compelling answer. Based on the verses we have examined in this chapter, do you think Jesus fits the definition of the word "poor"? In other words, do you think Jesus was *indigent, impoverished, needy, wanting in material goods, destitute, feeble, dejected, worthy of pity or sympathy, inferior, pitiful, second-class, second-rate, lacking,* or *insufficient?*

On the other hand, consider the definition of the word "prosperous" — *marked by success or economic well-being, enjoying vigorous and healthy growth, flourishing, successful, robust, progress-ing, favorable.*

Which definition best describes the biblical Jesus? Let's review the information about Jesus we discovered in God's Word:

As a child, Jesus received gifts of gold, frankincense, and myrrh.

Jesus had many partners who faithfully and consistently supported His ministry financially.

The Bible indicates that Jesus had a house or a residence.

When it was necessary, God's miraculous power operated through Jesus to see that His needs and the needs of others were met.

The Bible indicates that Jesus' ministry assisted the poor financially on a regular basis.

Jesus had a treasurer who regularly embezzled money from the funds entrusted to him.

Jesus distinguished Himself from the poor.

Jesus was not the least bit bothered when perfume worth a year's salary was used to anoint His feet.

The testimony of Jesus' own disciples at the end of His earthly ministry was that they never lacked anything.

When Jesus was crucified, His clothes were nice enough that the soldiers gambled for them.

I believe these scriptural facts are compelling proof that Jesus was not poor, but was a prosperous man. Now I am not suggesting that He lived a lavish or extravagant lifestyle — that would not have been practical for Him. But Jesus had His needs met during His life on earth, and He was able to do what God asked Him to do.

Jesus' prosperity should not surprise us. The Old Covenant promised prosperity to those who walked in the will of God (*see* Deuteronomy 29:9; Joshua 1:7; 1 Kings 2:3; 1 Chronicles 22:13; 2 Chronicles 20:20 and 26:5; Job 36:11; Nehemiah 1:11, and Psalm 1:1-3).

Do you think that Jesus met the qualification of walking in God's will? Of course, He did. He declared in John 6:38, *"For I came down from heaven, not to do Mine own will, but the will of Him that sent me."*

Do you think that the Father kept His Word and blessed Jesus because He walked in the Father's will? Absolutely! Numbers 23:19 says, *"God is not a man, that he should lie . . . hath he said, and shall he not do it? or hath he spoken, and shall he not make it good?"*

Jesus was not poor. He walked in prosperity according to the Abrahamic Covenant.

THE PURPOSE OF PROSPERITY

I have carefully explained to you why I believe Jesus was prosperous.

However, His prosperity was not measured by the accumulation of great wealth and worldly possessions. He did not live in a palace with rooms full of gold, looking out over fields of cattle and sheep. His lifestyle was not lavish or extravagant, and He was not driven by possessiveness and greed.

Yet in a small country dominated by Rome's mighty power, where the majority of the people were oppressed and exploited, Jesus' personal needs were met. He could afford to move around the country freely, going about His Father's business. He was even able to support a dozen disciples who traveled with Him throughout Galilee and into the neighboring regions.

Why did Jesus have such relatively abundant resources? Those resources enabled Him to do God's will. Perhaps you've heard the saying, "Where God guides, He provides." Well, I believe the purpose of prosperity for a Christian is to do God's work and God's will.

What is God's will? John 3:16 and 17 expresses it very simply: *"For God so loved the world, that he gave his only begotten Son, that whosoever believeth in him should not perish, but have everlasting life. For God sent not his Son into the world to condemn the world; but that the world through him might be saved."* God's primary interest is saving the lost! That's why He sent His Son.

The Bible is also very plain about what Jesus did when He came to earth. Matthew 9:35 says, *"And Jesus went about all the cities and villages, teaching in their synagogues, and preaching the gospel of the kingdom, and healing every sickness and every disease among the people."*

Jesus is our great example. What He did, we should do. His purpose should be our purpose. Jesus said, "I tell you the truth, anyone who has faith in me will do what I have been doing. He will do even greater things than these, because I am going to the Father" (John 14:12 *NIV*).

Establish Your Motives

Can we expect to be prosperous? Yes, we can, just as Jesus was. But that means that our motive for being prosperous should also be the same as His. He wants His people — including His preachers — to have plenty to enable them to go teach, preach, and heal people in the villages and cities of the world or to help others to go. In God's economy, prosperity is the means to an end — world evangelism.

Why do we want to prosper? Is it our desire to minister to others or to ourselves? Do we seek prosperity to help finance the work of God or to enjoy the luxuries of life — big houses, showy cars, expensive clothes, fancy food, and lavish entertainment?

I am not suggesting that God expects us to live on a skimpy, cramped, barely-get-by budget. Numerous Old Testament verses promise prosperity — an abundance or having more than enough — to those who do God's will. Psalm 35:27 says, ". . . *Let the Lord be magnified, which hath pleasure in the prosperity of his servant.*"

Is God magnified by your scraping along, living hand to mouth? No. Is He magnified if you are living extravagantly, focusing all your attention and time on money and worldly possessions? No. There must be balance and common sense in our material lives.

As we read the Gospels and study the life of Christ, we get the picture of a Man who walked the streets of the villages and towns where He went, paying His own way, mingling comfortably with the common people, and helping the poor. But He was also right at home visiting with the affluent and powerful. He went to the homes of Pharisees and the religious leaders, as well as the homes of sinners, like the tax collector, Zaccheus. Jesus' first recorded miracle took place at a wedding banquet in Cana, where He turned several large jars of water into wine for the feast (see John 2).

In the Sermon on the Mount, Jesus taught that we do not have to worry about food, drink, or clothing. Jesus said, ". . . *for your heavenly Father knoweth that ye have need of all these things. But seek ye first the kingdom of God, and his righteousness; AND ALL THESE THINGS SHALL BE ADDED UNTO YOU*" (Matt. 6:32,33). He went on to say, "Give, and it will be given to you. A good measure, pressed down, shaken together and running over, will be poured into your lap. For with the measure you use, it will be measured to you" (Luke 6:38 *NIV*).

Does that sound like God wants to limit how much we can have? Absolutely not. He simply wants us to keep our priorities straight. Philippians 4:19 says, *"But my God shall supply all your need according to his riches in glory by Christ Jesus."* We've already discovered that God's riches are absolutely unlimited; everything belongs to Him.

Paul urged the Church at Corinth to give generously and cheerfully to God's work. Then he went on to say, "God is able to make it up to you by giving you everything you need and more, so that there will not only be enough for your own needs, but plenty left over to give joyfully to others" (2 Cor. 9:8 *TLB*).

God's People Must Prosper To Fulfill the Great Commission

As Christians, we can expect to be blessed and to prosper if we seek prosperity as a means to help accomplish God's will and purpose. Jesus said about Himself, *"For the Son of man is come to seek and to save that which was lost"* (Luke 19:10).

Jesus has commissioned all believers to carry out the same mission. In Mark 16:15, He declares, *". . . Go ye into all the world, and preach the gospel to every creature."* That seems clear enough — you go into all the world and preach the Gospel to every creature! With more than six billion people in the world today, we have a mighty big job left to do. We certainly need to walk in prosperity in order to have the funds to get it done.

Jesus also pointed out that we need the power of the Holy Ghost in our lives to carry out His Great Commission. Acts 1:8 says, *"But ye shall receive power, after that the Holy Ghost is come upon you: and ye shall be witnesses unto me both in Jerusalem, and in all Judaea, and in Samaria, and unto the uttermost part of the earth."*

How are we supposed to go about fulfilling the Great Commission? First, we should start in our Jerusalem, or our hometown. Jerusalem was home to most of the one hundred twenty who gathered in the Upper Room on the Day of Pentecost. Then, second, we are to be witnesses in our region, our Judaea, and in the region next to us, or our Samaria. Finally, we are to take the Gospel to the uttermost part of the earth.

One thing is obvious: Poverty-stricken people are limited in their ability to fulfill the Great Commission. Without funds, they have difficulty going into all the world and neither can they help send someone else. So if God requires every believer to help carry out this mission, then it must be His plan and His will for His people to prosper.

Throughout the Bible, God's work typically has been financed by the tithes and gifts of His people. The tithe is ten percent of the harvest or of the gain or increase received. The giving of God's people took care of God's house and those who worked there and provided the funds to carry out His work on earth.

Perhaps the most familiar Bible text on the subject of tithes is found in the Book of Malachi.

"Bring the whole tithe into the storehouse, that there may be food in my house. Test me in this," says the Lord Almighty, "and see if I will not throw open the floodgates of heaven and pour out so much blessing that you will not have room enough for it. I will prevent pests from devouring your crops, and the vines in your fields will not cast their fruit," says the Lord Almighty. "Then all the nations will call you blessed, for yours will be a delightful land," says the Lord Almighty.

— Malachi 3:10-12 (NIV)

We see from this scripture that tithing is linked to prosperity. The Word of God says that if we tithe on our income to the Lord, He will pour out blessings without measure. Notice that God said He would bless the tither in two ways — in an abundance of increase and in protecting his goods from being spoiled. Malachi 3:11 in the *King James Version* says, *"And I will rebuke the devourer for your sakes. . . ."*

Tithing — God's Plan for Financing
The Church and Its Outreaches

Why do we experience such a blessing when we pay ten percent of our income back to God? It's certainly not because He needs the money or anything else we could offer Him. No, tithing is a powerful way to plug in to what God is doing in the world. The combined tithe of a congregation provides the funds to support the outreaches of a church — getting people saved, building up the Body of Christ, ministering to the poor, supporting missions, perhaps sponsoring the Gospel on radio or television, and helping to provide a living for the pastor and ministry staff.

As a general principle, I believe people should tithe to their local church. I have always believed and taught that the local church is the primary means that God uses to bless people in the earth. The local church is where the saints are cared for, and it is to be the base for all other outreaches.

Various other ministries can and should be supported by offerings and other forms of financial support that come from individuals and churches. But in most situations, the tithe should go to the local church.

Being able to have a part in God's plan is the reason and purpose for paying our tithes and giving our offerings. Realizing that we can become a partner with God in carrying out His will brings great fulfillment and satisfaction — mentally, emotionally, and spiritually. And it also opens the windows of Heaven for an outpouring of material blessings.

One of the most interesting teachings on tithing I've found came from a book entitled *The Path to Wealth*, published in 1888 by T. S. Linscott. He said the following:

> It is a singular fact that all the blessings we get, temporal and spiritual, come from the heavens. There are three heavens; one where the birds fly, or our atmosphere; another where the sun, moon and stars are; and the other where God dwells. All our temporal blessings; all our national and individual prosperity; all material wealth; in a word, all our riches come from the earth and the heavens; and, inasmuch as the yield of the earth depends wholly upon the air, the dew, the rain and sunshine of the heavens, we can say practically, that all our temporal blessings come from heaven. Now, God pledges himself to open the windows of heaven and pour us out the divinest blessings — overflowing blessings, "heaped up, pressed down, shaken together, running over," that "there shall not be room enough to receive it."
>
> Here is God's direct pledge for temporal blessings; and I am simple enough to believe it, and intend to comply with the conditions and risk the consequences. It is a very easy thing for God to withhold or grant temporal

prosperity. Stored up in the heavens is enough wealth to make every living man rich; and my God, whose pledge I have, can at any time open a little window and let down upon me a gentle shower of his blessings, which will provide for me and mine so long as we need temporal good. "Trust in the Lord and do good, so shalt thou dwell in the land, and verily thou shalt be fed." "He that watereth shall be watered also himself." "Honor the Lord with thy substance, and with the firstfruits of all thine increase, so shall thy barns be filled with plenty, and thy presses shall burst out with new wine." These are rich and precious promises, and they will be fulfilled only when we comply with the conditions and pay our tenth to God.

A good deal of our preaching, our thinking, and even our devotions, either vaporize or spiritualize God's promises. Our natural unbelief tends to put off the fulfilment of them until we get to heaven, or to some time in the future. Unbelief hates literal and present tense promises. But these promises are literal and material; they are for here and now; they are to be enjoyed on earth; they challenge us to a contract or bargain with God. As stated before, He promises money for money; you pay me a tenth, says God, and I will give you earthly and material blessings. I will give your fingers skill as mechanics; I will incline employers towards you; you shall get the highest wages; strikes shall not affect you; I am with you, and will see that you are provided for.

I will make you prosperous as business men; I will incline you where you can make good bargains; I will send the people around you to buy; while the man next door, who neglects my cause, may become bankrupt, this curse shall not touch you. I will look out for your bills when they are coming due; I will see that your bank account is sufficiently large; in a word, I am your partner and will look out for the interests of your business.

And to you thinkers, who earn your living by your brains, I will make your thoughts clear; I will give you the holy impulse to originate "thoughts which breathe, and words which burn"; your productions shall stir men's hearts; your work shall be in demand; I will make people buy the productions of your heart and brain; only pay me your tenth, and you shall be cared for.

Seed time and harvest shall never fail you farmers; I will bless your crops; I will multiply your stock; the blight and the mildew shall be kept from your farms; remember, I am the God of Abraham, Isaac and Jacob; I will do to you as I did to them, only remember me as they did.

I will give health to all of you; death shall not take away your little ones; they shall live to a ripe old age; I will open the windows of heaven and pour you out a blessing that there shall not be room enough to receive it. These are blessings promised by God in the Bible. Who among this company will this day pledge his tenth to God?

As intimated just now, this wonderful blessing promised in this passage of Scripture, and in other passages of Scripture, as a reward of obedience, is more than mere temporal prosperity. Not only will God open the windows of heaven from whence comes material wealth, but he will open the windows of the upper heavens where He dwells, the centre of the universe; and from His gracious fullness He will shed down upon those who are obedient, blessings which are inexpressible and full of glory.[1]

Understand Why and How You Should Tithe

About fifty years ago, I was pastoring a church in the oil fields of east Texas. One of the deacons of the church had a good job working for Humble Oil Company. And he was always faithful in his support of the church.

One day he said to me, "Brother Hagin, can you explain something to me? I've been a Christian for thirteen years, and I've been faithful in paying my tithes and giving offerings."

I knew that was true. He was a regular tither whose support really blessed the church. "What is it you want to know?" I asked.

He said, "Well, I don't know why I'm doing it. I've never heard any teaching or preaching about tithing. When I got saved, they told me I was supposed to do it, so I did. But I don't know of anything that's ever come of it in thirteen years. If I've ever gotten any blessing out of it, I don't know it."

I was amazed. Here was a good man who had been tithing strictly from the standpoint of slavish duty, and it hadn't worked for him. So I took a few minutes and told him a little bit of what I'm sharing with you in this chapter.

Then I said to him, "The next time you get your tithe envelope out, say, 'Lord, I'm doing this by faith. I'm giving for the purpose of keeping this local church going, which is benefiting the Body of Christ by helping people. I'm helping spread the Gospel so that people can be saved. Thank You, God, for making it possible for me to be part of Your work. I am giving in faith and expectancy to be blessed according to Your Word.'"

"I'll sure give that a try," he said. And he did.

About thirty days later, he came back to me with a big grin on his face. "I've been doing what you said, Brother Hagin. Every week I've been praying when I get ready to pay my tithes. And boy," he declared, "it's really working. I can definitely tell a difference in my finances!"

Another time, in another east Texas church, a man came to me and said, "Brother Hagin, my wife and I have been paying tithes ever since we got saved, nearly twenty-five years. But we've never heard any teaching from the Bible about it. Many of our friends in the church are farmers. They borrow money to buy seed to plant, and when the cotton is ready, they hire people to pick it. How do they pay tithes?

"I talked to one or two of the deacons," he said. "And they don't know much about it, either. They said they had thought about asking you to preach about it, but they didn't want you to think they were trying to tell you what to preach. So I wanted to see if you thought you would be talking about it anytime soon?"

I said to the man, "Brother Williams, I'm glad you brought this up. God has been dealing with me about this before you ever said anything. So I'm going to do it right away."

In those days, the biggest crowd we had at our church was on Sunday night. The building was usually full, and if the weather was good, sometimes there would be people standing outside. Because I wanted the most people possible to hear what the Bible says about tithing and giving, I took a Sunday night and spent about an hour on the subject, going into great detail.

I had always tried to preach a balanced message to the church. I had preached about salvation, the baptism of the Holy Ghost, and the gifts of the Spirit. I had preached about healing, faith, and living a life of love and service to others. So the people knew I wasn't trying to cram something down their throats when I preached about finances; it was something they needed and wanted to know.

After the service, many of the folks told me how glad they were that I had preached about tithing and giving — that I had helped them understand what the Bible said and the purpose for giving to God. I could tell they had taken it to heart.

Tithing Brings the Promised Blessings of God

Well, immediately the income of the church tripled! Without any special emphasis or pull, there was a generous response when we passed the offering plate. Even sinners started paying their tithes. There were two ladies in the church who were married to unsaved men. These two men would come to church with their families on Sunday night.

The very next day after I preached on tithing, one of these men stopped by the parsonage. "Brother Hagin," he said. "My wife and I talked about your sermon on the way home last night. We believe that God will bless us if we obey His Word.

I just got off my first bales of cotton so I wanted to stop by and pay our tithes."

Well, those unsaved fellows kept on paying their tithes. And it wasn't long until both of them got saved and filled with the Spirit. Their families were blessed too. Later, one of the wives was called to preach, and the family went out on the field to minister. The last account I had of them, they were traveling about and evangelizing.

In my more than sixty-five years of ministry, I've heard thousands of testimonies from people who have practiced God's biblical plan of returning a tenth of their income to Him through the local church. A great many of them, in the beginning, weren't sure how they could get by on the remaining ninety percent of their income when they had been barely making it beforehand. But somehow they did. Oh, it wasn't always easy. It required patience, determination, faith, and some time.

But if they persisted, the promised blessings came. Sometimes they noticed that God had "rebuked the devourer" in their lives — the car or the appliances didn't break down as often or the kids weren't sick as much, resulting in fewer medical bills. If they worked in construction or as farmers, bad weather didn't keep them off the job. Then many times, extra income would come from totally unexpected sources. Perhaps they would get a raise, some overtime hours, or maybe even a bonus! Others reported that they got an insurance settlement, collected on an old debt, or received an inheritance.

The bottom line was that when they paid their tithes, they had more financially and did better. And most people were also blessed spiritually with a closer walk with God, physically with better health, and mentally and emotionally with a greater sense of joy and well-being. The Bible says, *"The blessing of the Lord, it maketh rich, and he addeth no sorrow with it"* (Prov. 10:22).

To Tithe or Not To Tithe

From time to time over the years, people have asked me if the practice of tithing is still valid for the Church today. "The New Testament really says very little about it," they say. "Should pastors and other ministers preach and encourage tithing with so little New Testament information on the subject. Should Christians be bound by the Old Testament Law?"

It is true that there is very little mention of tithing in the New Testament. Two of the Gospels, Matthew and Luke, report the only recorded incident of Jesus saying anything about it. But in this instance, Jesus clearly affirmed His belief in the practice of tithing:

> *"Yes, woe upon you, Pharisees, and you other religious leaders — hypocrites! For you tithe down to the last mint leaf in your garden, but ignore the important things —*

justice and mercy and faith. Yes, you should tithe, but

you shouldn't leave the more important things undone."

— Matthew 23:23 (TLB)

Jesus upbraided the hypocritical religious leaders of His day who ignored vitally important parts of the Law such a justice, mercy, and faith, while meticulously paying the tithe they owed down to the last leaf in their garden. He was saying that giving money doesn't take the place of living right. God is not as interested in a person's money as He is in his heart. But Jesus did say that a person should tithe.

Although the majority of biblical references to the tithe are clearly part of the Old Covenant, the fact of the matter is that tithing was not introduced under the Law. It was merely regulated under the Law. Tithing originated as an act of faith, and faith transcends both the Old and New Covenants! And "by faith" is how we should tithe today — not as an act of legalism, but as an act of faith.

Genesis chapter 14 tells us how Abram paid tithes to Melchizedek, king of Salem and a priest of the Most High God, four hundred years before the time of Moses and the Law. Obviously, he did not pay tithes by legalistic requirement because he lived before the Law. Isaac and Jacob also lived before the Law and paid tithes (Gen. 18:19,20;28:22).

By faith, Abraham paid tithes to Melchizedek, the priest of the Most High God, who was a type of Christ. We see this in the Book of Hebrews, which also tells us that, ". . . Jesus has become the guarantee of a better covenant" (Heb. 7:22 NIV).

Galatians chapter 3 makes some crucially important statements.

> But that no man is justified by the law in the sight of God, it is evident: for, The just shall live by faith. And the law is not of faith: but, The man that doeth them shall live in them. Christ hath redeemed us from the curse of the law, being made a curse for us: for it is written, Cursed is every one that hangeth on a tree: That the blessing of Abraham might come on the Gentiles through Jesus Christ; that we might receive the promise of the Spirit through faith.
>
> — Galatians 3:11-14

So should we pay tithes today? Absolutely! But we pay them like Abraham paid them — not by the Law, but by faith. And besides that, if the people of God paid ten percent *before* the Law and ten percent *under* the Law, should we, who live by grace, be doing any less when we have a better covenant?

Abraham paid tithes to Melchizedek, the priest of the Most High God, who was a type of Christ. And he received the blessing, which was threefold — spiritual, physical, and material or financial. Because we are redeemed from the curse of the Law by the sacrifice of Christ, we have received the blessing of Abraham — spiritually, physically, and financially.

We, then, by faith follow the example of Abraham in paying tithes. We pay our tithes unto Christ! The Bible says in Ephesians that when God raised Jesus from the dead, He gave Him to be the Head over all things to the Church, which is His Body (Eph. 1:22,23). So when we pay tithes to Christ, the Head, they flow to His Body, the Church. Do you see it? Through the Church, we have the great privilege of giving to Jesus to do His will and work.

I believe if every Christian would be faithful in tithing and giving, there would be more than enough funds for the Church to carry out its mission in the world. Researchers have found that amazingly few born-again Americans tithe regularly, and a surprisingly large number give *nothing*! Imagine what could be accomplished if all Christians were faithful in their tithing and giving!

More Money Results in More Ministry

Years ago, I was part of an association called the Voice of Healing, which was founded by Gordon Lindsay, a great man of God and a marvelous writer. The organization is now known as Christ for the Nations. Lindsay wrote the following back in 1961, and it is still extremely pertinent:

The main hindrance to world evangelization has not been for the want of devoted missionaries, nor is it the lack for trained nationals, which was a serious problem for many years. The hour has come when we have an eager army of gospel soldiers ready to launch out in faith and to preach the apostolic gospel. And they are doing it! Nor is there a lack of people responding to the message. Any missionary will tell you that almost every place an evangelistic effort is attempted, hundreds and in many cases even thousands will respond. Where then is the lack? It is in the lack of necessary financial assistance that often is not available at the moment the Spirit of God moves in a community.[2]

How much more could your church be doing to minister in your city, in your community, in our nation, and around the world if more funds were available? Suppose your church's income was suddenly multiplied by four. Could it have a greater impact in reaching more souls, ministering to more saints, helping more poor people, or financing more missionaries? How many projects have remained in the dreaming or planning stage because the money to make them into a reality was never available?

Let's look at another section of T. S. Linscott's 1888 book, *The Path to Wealth*:

We find the Church of God descending to business methods in order to raise money enough to pay its expenses; hence, we have tea-meetings, bazaars, concerts . . . and all sorts of schemes to raise money; while the vast majority rob God of His tithes, and hypocritically sing:

"Were the whole realm of nature mine,

That were a present far too small;

Love so amazing, so divine,

Demands my soul, my life, my all."

If Christian people would live up to the Bible demand, and pay God one-tenth of their income, there would be no need for such methods of raising money — there would be enough and to spare; and I believe the Millennium would soon be upon us; for the conversion of the world is, in my opinion, now reduced to a question of money. We have the men and women whose hearts God has touched, and whose souls are aflame with missionary zeal; we have a Gospel that meets the requirements of all sorts and conditions of men; full provision has been made for the salvation of the world.

For whosoever shall call upon the name of the Lord shall be saved. How then shall they call on him in whom they have not believed? and how shall they believe in him of whom they have not heard? and how shall they hear without a preacher? And how shall they preach, except they be sent? . . .

— Romans 10:13-15

And how can they be sent without money? And how can they get the money except it be given them in God's appointed way, by the tithes of the people "who have heard the joyful sound?"[3]

Those are challenging thoughts. And I believe they are just as timely and appropriate today as they were more than a hundred years ago when they were first published.

Partnership With God

Through tithing to our local church and giving offerings to other worthy ministries, we can be part of what God is doing in the world today. Our motive and purpose for giving should be pure and unselfish.

1. *We should do it because we love God.* Giving is a natural expression of love. John 3:16 says, "God so loved the world that He gave." And we should do the same; we should give to God because we love Him.

2. *We should give to God in obedience to His Word.* The Bible teaches us to give to the Lord and support His work. In addition to the scriptures we've already examined, there are

many others that are unmistakable in their instruction about giving.

3. *We should give as a means to help carry out Christ's Great Commission* and support the work of those who are going into all the world with the Gospel.

4. *We should give because we want to see people blessed.* Our tithes and gifts help support outreaches of the local church and other organizations that minister to the poor, evangelize the lost and unreached, and build up the saints while equipping them for Christian service.

5. *And, finally, way down the line, we should give in expectancy,* believing God to honor the promises in His Word to bless and prosper us. Notice that I have listed five reasons to give, and I believe the order of this list reflects priorities that are very important. It seems to me that many preachers are overemphasizing *number five* and presenting that as the major reason for people to give.

Nevertheless, giving is a tried and proven way to plant seeds for a harvest that will result in our needs being met. The law of sowing and reaping does apply in the area of personal finances. The Bible is true when it says, "Give, *and it shall be given unto you; good measure, pressed down, and shaken together, and running over, shall men give into your bosom. . .*" (Luke 6:38).

All of these are good and valid reasons for giving. And I believe they will lead to true prosperity — spirit, soul, and body.

---

[1]Thomas Samuel Linscott, *The Path to Wealth*, B. F. Johnson, Richmond, Va., 1888, pp. 106-110.

[2]Gordon Lindsay, *God's 20th Century Barnabas*, Christ for the Nations, Inc., Dallas, 1982, p. 235. Used by permission.

[3]Linscott, pp. 60-61.

CHAPTER FIVE

SHOULD PREACHERS PROSPER?

Misunderstandings about money have hurt a lot of Christians over the years — both ministers and lay people.

Over the centuries, the Church has managed to either be in the ditch on one side of the road or the other from time to time regarding this subject. Yet the Word of God gives clear, specific teaching about supporting the work of the ministry and those called of God to minister.

From my personal experience in more than sixty-five years of ministry, I've observed churches that failed to adequately provide for the needs of their pastors. Too many congregations have kept their pastors poor and impoverished, not having the same average standard of living as the members enjoyed.

I've seen some ministers flounder because of their lack of finances. Their personal testimonies suffered because they weren't able to pay their bills. Those who saw a minister who was so obviously financially downtrodden didn't want to be part of his church. And the more the church withheld from its pastor, the worse it did financially — the greater lack it experienced.

In my five decades on the evangelistic field, I've always encouraged local congregations to take good care of their pastors. And in every case I know about, those that did take care of their pastors flourished and prospered, spiritually as well as financially.

On the other hand, there have been some preachers — a minority of pastors, evangelists, and other ministers — who abused their position and influence to seek exorbitant personal financial gain over all else. Their greedy, manipulative efforts have hurt the Body of Christ and given unbelieving critics ammunition to attack and discredit God's work.

It's high time for ministers and believers today to get out of both ditches of error and back in the middle of the high road that God intended for us to travel. While biblical prosperity for all believers has a solid scriptural foundation, wrong motives and misuse of these truths can create stumbling blocks that cause offense and injury to many.

Caring for the Messenger

The Bible has plenty to say in both the Old and New Testaments about how ministers are to be supported. One of the most important and enlightening passages is found in the Apostle Paul's first letter to the Church at Corinth.

. . . What soldier at any time serves at his own expense? Who plants a vineyard and does not eat any of the fruit of it? Who tends a flock and does not partake of the milk of the flock? Do I say this only on human authority and as a man reasons? Does not the Law endorse the same principle? For in the Law of Moses it is written, You shall not muzzle an ox when it is treading out the corn. Is it [only] for oxen that God cares? Or does He speak certainly and entirely for our sakes? [Assuredly] it is written for our sakes, because the plowman ought to plow in hope, and the thresher ought to thresh in expectation of partaking of the harvest. If we have sown [the seed of] spiritual good among you, [is it too] much if we reap from your material benefits? . . . Do you not know that those men who are employed in the services of the temple get their food from the temple? And that those who

tend the altar share with the altar [in the offerings brought]? [On the same principle] the Lord directed that those who publish the good news (the Gospel) should live (get their maintenance) by the Gospel.

— 1 Corinthians 9:7-11,13,14 (*Amplified*)

Another translation of verse 14 says, "On the same principle the Lord has ordered that those who proclaim the gospel should receive their livelihood from those who accept the gospel" (*Phillips*).

Galatians 6:6 reinforces the same truth: "Let him who receives instruction in the Word [of God] share all good things with his teacher [contributing to his support]" (*Amplified*). The Phillips translation of this verse says, "The man under Christian instruction should be willing to contribute toward the livelihood of his teacher."

First Timothy 5:17 in *The Living Bible* says, "Pastors who do their work well should be paid well and should be highly appreciated, especially those who work hard at both preaching and teaching." The Williams translation says, "Elders who do their duties well should be considered as deserving twice the salary they get, especially those who keep on toiling in preaching and teaching."

So the Word of God makes it clear that ministers of the Gospel should be well supported by those they minister to.

That has been the practice and pattern for centuries according to the direction and instruction of the Lord.

Today in America many ministers on church pastoral staffs are paid a salary and provided with basic benefits, very much like people in other professions. I think that generally this is a healthy situation because it helps insure that the preacher's income is not influenced or dependent upon what he preaches about. On occasion, however, the people may choose to bless their pastor with a love offering or other special gift.

Tithes and Offerings in the 1930s and '40s

When I was a pastor, the common practice in most Full Gospel churches was to take the tithes and offerings received on Sunday morning and give them to the pastor as his income. The offerings on Sunday night and at the midweek service went to pay the overhead and expenses of the church. Sometimes additional offerings were received for special projects, missions, or other outreaches. During revival meetings, offerings were received each night either to support the evangelist or to cover the church's additional expenses.

My weekly income as a pastor averaged about $45 a month. Remember, this was during the 1930s and '40s. Although I knew that many of the people in my congregation were not paying a tithe of their income, I never tried to make an issue of it. I taught what the Bible says about tithing and giving, but was careful not to overemphasize just that part of the Christian message.

If the Sunday morning tithes and offerings ran short, I would quickly feel the pinch. After a week or two of receiving less than my basic operating budget, I would find myself unable to make my Montgomery Ward or Sears and Roebuck payment and still put gas in the car and feed my family.

So I would get up before the church on a Sunday night and say, "Folks, I'm going to take up an extra offering tonight for the pastor. Now we all know that if everybody paid their tithes, there would be plenty of money for my needs and the church's needs. We could build a new church building and a new parsonage. But not enough is coming in to meet the needs. I'm not fussing at you, but I need such-and-such amount to pay my bills." Almost always various people would start speaking out, saying they would give a dollar or fifty cents. In no time the need would be met. Then I would probably never mention the subject again until the next time my income fell below budget.

I could have concentrated on raising my support each week by teaching on giving and making a "pull" at offering time. But I never felt comfortable doing that. I believed then — and now — that constantly focusing on just one topic or theme was not in the best interest of the people. My responsibility was to bless and help the people, to meet all their needs. And that meant preaching the full Gospel — the whole counsel of the Word of God.

Present a Balanced Message

Very early in my ministry, the Lord dealt with me about the crucial importance of the faith message, saying, "Go teach my people faith." Some have supposed that from that time on, all I did was talk about faith. But that's not so. While I always included an emphasis on faith when it was appropriate, I felt constrained to present the whole Gospel, a balanced message.

I've known pastors who have focused more on money, giving, and prosperity than any other subject. Sometimes they would put a guilt trip on people if they didn't give, or they would use high-pressure tactics to motivate individuals to respond.

I've never felt that was the right way to present this important truth to the people of God. Yes, I know all the scripture verses that teach both the responsibility and blessing of giving. The Bible does say, "*Give, and it shall be given unto you . . .*" (Luke 6:38). It does say, "*. . . seek ye first the kingdom of God, and his righteousness; and all these things shall be added unto you*" (Matthew 6:33). These truths definitely should be taught to all believers. But the Word also says, *"Every man according as he pur-poseth in his heart, so let him give; not grudgingly, or of necessity: for God loveth a cheerful giver"* (2 Cor. 9:7).

Another rendering of that passage says, "I want each of you to take plenty of time to think it over, and make up your own mind what you will give. That will protect you against sob stories and arm-twisting. God loves it when the giver delights in the giving" (*Message*).

I've also heard preachers try to hammer Christians by quoting from Malachi chapter 3 saying that they are *cursed* if they don't pay tithes and give offerings. Obviously, this is not correct. While the people of Malachi's day were under the Law of Moses, the New Testament plainly declares that Christ has redeemed us from the curse of the Law (Gal. 3:13).

Does that mean that tithing is no longer valid? Not at all. As I said in the last chapter, God's people were tithers four hundred years *before* the Law, and Jesus reaffirmed the validity of tithing in His teaching. In the only recorded instance of Jesus' referring to tithing, He said it should be done!

But there is no curse today for not tithing. We are free from the legalistic requirements of the Mosaic Law. Is there any other consequence? Yes, if we don't tithe, we limit our-selves from receiving the blessings God has promised those who pay tithes and give offerings by faith.

Giving is an essential part of Christian living. Every Christian leader has a responsibility to practice and teach what the Bible says about giving. But the emphasis must be kept in balance with teachings about other truths and doctrines in the Word of God. Pastors do as much a disservice to their congregations by *never* teaching on tithing and giving as by talking about it *all the time*. There must be balance. And the purpose for the instruction must be for the benefit and blessing of the people — not just for what the preacher will gain from it.

The Bible says that Jesus went about teaching, preaching, and healing (Matt. 9:35). It doesn't say that He spent a lot of time taking up offerings and emphasizing prosperity. We know He did have partners who supported His ministry. We can find scripture references where Jesus talked about money and giving, especially in reference to helping the poor. But even the critics of Jesus were never able to say that He was in it for the money. Instead, the report that was published throughout all Judaea was that He went about doing good and healing all that were oppressed of the devil (Acts 10:38).

Consider the Qualifications of a Pastor

Being responsible in seeking financial support for God's work is an awesome charge for those called to ministry. Cicero, a great Roman statesman who died a few years before the birth of Christ, said, "But the chief thing in all public administra-tion and public service is to avoid even the slightest suspicion of self-seeking." If this is true of public servants, how much more should it apply to God's servants.

The Bible gives a list of qualifications for those who would seek the pastoral office. First Timothy 3:2 and 3 says, "A *bishop* [pastor] *then must be blameless, the husband of one wife, vigilant, sober, of good behaviour, given to hospitality, apt to teach; not given to wine, no striker, not greedy of filthy lucre* [money]; *but patient, not a brawler, not covetous."*

The Amplified Bible makes the point even stronger. First Timothy 3:3 says, ". . . not a lover of money [insatiable for wealth and ready to obtain it by questionable means]."

So while it is absolutely proper for a pastor or other min-ister to expect adequate financial support, he must not go overboard and spend all of his time and effort seeking person-al financial gain. The danger is not in having money or things, but in becoming covetous. The lie of covetousness says, "If only I had a little more money or a few more material posses-sions, I would be happy." But that's not true, because usually the more people get, the more they want.

Hebrews 13:5 says, "*Let your conversation be without cov-etousness.* . . ." In the Greek, the word translated "conversation" here really means *conduct or manner of life.* So the passage is saying, "Let your conduct be without covetousness." Verse 5 continues, ". . . *and be content with such things as ye have: for he hath said, I will never leave thee, nor forsake thee.*"

The Phillips translation bears this out, saying, "Keep your lives free from the lust for money: be content with what you have."

Look at the emphasis found in *The Amplified Bible.*

Let your character or moral disposition be free from love of money [including greed, avarice, lust, and craving for earthly possessions] and be satisfied with your present [circumstances and with what you have]; for He [God] Himself has said, I will not in any way fail you nor give you up nor leave you without support. [I will] not, [I will] not, [I will] not in any degree leave you helpless nor forsake nor let [you] down (relax My hold on you)! [Assuredly not!]

— Hebrews 13:5 (*Amplified*)

Run From the Love of Money

How dangerous is covetousness, especially the lust for money? The Word of God is abundantly clear about it, warning all — both ministers and lay people alike. First Timothy 6:10 says, "*For the love of money is the root of all evil: which while some coveted after, they have erred from the faith, and pierced themselves through with many sorrows."* Notice that it doesn't say that *money* is the root of all evil, which many have mistakenly taught, but that *the love of money* — or covetousness — is the root of all evil.

In fact, the Apostle Paul under the anointing of the Holy Ghost wrote this letter to the young minister, Timothy. He emphasized the fact that "things" in themselves are not bad. And he charged Timothy to warn rich people not to trust in their riches but in God. Notice what First Timothy 6:17 says: *"Charge them that are rich in this world, that they be not high-minded, nor trust in uncertain riches, but in the living God, who giveth us richly all things to enjoy."*

So things — even riches — are gifts from God, given for our enjoyment! We should enjoy the good things of life, but we must never allow the gifts we enjoy to become more important than the Giver!

What if someone — even a preacher — deliberately leaves the main road of truth and gets off in the ditch of error? The Bible says to get away from that person! First Timothy 6:5 says, *"Perverse disputings of men of corrupt minds, and destitute of the truth, supposing that gain is godliness: from such withdraw thyself."*

The Amplified Bible says such individuals, ". . . imagine that godliness or righteousness is a source of profit [a money-making business, a means of livelihood]. From such withdraw" (1 Tim. 6:5).

In First Timothy 6:11, Paul gives advice to Timothy and to us: *"But thou, O man of God, flee these things. . . ."* As one modern-language version puts it, "But you, Timothy, man of God: Run for your life from all this. Pursue a righteous life — a life of wonder, faith, love, steadiness, courtesy. Run hard and fast in the faith" (1 Tim. 6:11,12 *Message*).

Years ago, I attended a crusade service conducted by a minister who was part of the healing revival. He was a gifted preacher who knew how to build faith and motivate people to expect and receive the healing power of the Lord. On that particular night, the anointing for healing was flowing in a mighty way, and several deaf people were healed — one right after the other. Everyone was aware of the mighty move of God that was going on, and there was a great surge of joy and excitement in that place.

Suddenly, the minister stopped and said, "We're going to receive a special offering." Although there had already been one offering earlier in the service, the minister obviously decided to take advantage of the high tide of emotionalism. He said, "We're not going to pass the offering plate again, but if you have a special gift, you can bring it down to me here at the front. Don't come unless you're going to bring at least $50!"

I watched as people almost ran over each other hurrying down to give him their $50. My spirit was grieved as I saw what was happening. Those people were not giving because they had purposed in their heart to help the Gospel go forth or to see other people healed. I don't believe they were giving it any thought or prayerful consideration at all.

Rather, they were caught up in the emotional outburst. Wanting to be part of the thrill and excitement of the moment, they were manipulated and exploited by this minister. I wondered how those people felt later on about what had happened when their emotions had settled back down. I can't help believing that at least some of them felt used and abused. I believe some of them later said to themselves, *I couldn't afford to give that $50. I didn't take time to think about it, and I shouldn't have done it.*

In my fifty years of field ministry while I was holding meetings across the nation, I deliberately chose never to receive an offering when the emotions of the people were highly charged. If there was a lot of excitement and exuberance when it was time for the offering, I would put it off until the mood had settled down.

I believe giving should be a conscious action that is done on purpose in a prayerful, thoughtful attitude. A minister should never resort to heavy persuasion, pleading, or pressure to push people into giving. Using gimmicks or making unrealistic promises is improper and out of order. A person's decision to give to God should never be something he will regret later.

My Directive From the Lord

In September 1950, I had a dramatic spiritual experience that made a tremendous impact on my life and ministry. I had a vision in which the Lord Jesus Christ appeared to me and gave me specific direction and instructions. In the next pages I want to tell about that divinely granted appearance.

At the time of this experience, I was conducting a tent revival in Rockwall, Texas, during the latter part of August and the first part of September 1950. On Saturday, September 2, it rained all day — not a hard, driving rain, but a slow, gentle, soaking rain.

It was still raining that evening at church time, and when we arrived at the tent, there were only about forty people present.

Rockwall is in the blackland of northcentral Texas, and there is a saying that if you stick with the blackland when it is dry, it will stick with you when it is wet. Many of the people who had been attending the meetings lived in the country, and they couldn't get out to the service that night because of the rain and mud. That's why the crowd was small.

Because everyone present was a Christian, I gave a Bible lesson and then invited the people to come to the front to pray. It was about 9:30 p.m. (Let me say here that I no more expected what was to follow than I expected to be the first man to land on the moon! I hadn't been praying that I would have such an experience. In fact, I hadn't even thought about such a thing.)

Everyone was praying around the front, and I knelt on the platform beside a folding chair near the pulpit. I began to pray in other tongues, and I heard a voice say, "Come up hither." At first, I didn't realize that the voice was speaking to me. I thought everyone heard it.

I See Jesus

"Come up hither," the voice said again. Then I looked and saw Jesus standing where the top of the tent would be. As I looked up again, the tent had disappeared, the folding chairs had disappeared, every tent pole had disappeared, the pulpit had disappeared, and God permitted me to see into the spirit realm.

Jesus was standing there, and I stood in His Presence. He was holding a crown in His hands. This crown was so extraordinarily beautiful that human language cannot begin to describe it.

Jesus told me, "This is a soulwinner's crown. My people are so careless and indifferent. This crown is for every one of My children. I speak and say, 'Go speak to this one or pray for that one,' but My people are too busy. They put it off, and souls are lost because they will not obey Me."

When Jesus said that, I wept before Him. I knelt down and repented of my failures. Then Jesus said to me again, "Come up hither." It seemed as if I went with Him through the air until we came to a beautiful city. We did not actually go into the city, but we beheld it at close range as one might go up on a mountain and look down on a city in the valley. Its beauty was beyond words!

Jesus said that people selfishly say they are ready for Heaven. They talk about their mansions and the glories of Heaven while many around them live in darkness and hopelessness. Jesus said I should share my hope with them and invite them to come to Heaven with me.

Then Jesus turned to me and said, "Now let us go down to hell."

We came back down out of Heaven, and when we got to earth we didn't stop, but kept on going. Numerous scriptures in the Bible refer to hell as being beneath us. For example, *"Hell from beneath is moved for thee to meet thee at thy coming. . . thou shalt be brought down to hell. . ."* (Isa. 14:9,15). *"Therefore hell hath enlarged herself. . .and he. . .shall descend into it"* (Isa. 5:14).

We went down to hell, and as we went into that place, I saw what appeared to be human beings wrapped in flames. I said, "Lord, this looks just like it did when I died and came to this place on April 22, 1933. You spoke, and I came back up out of here. I then repented and prayed, seeking Your forgiveness, and You saved me. Only now I feel so different: I am neither afraid nor horrified, as I was then."

Jesus told me, "Warn men and women about this place," and I cried out with tears that I would.

He then brought me back to earth. I became aware that I was kneeling on the platform by the folding chair and Jesus was standing by my side. As He stood there, He talked to me about my ministry. He told me some things in general that He later explained in more detail in another vision. Then Jesus disappeared, and I realized I was still kneeling on the platform. I could hear people praying all around me.

The Throne of God

A few minutes later I again saw Jesus standing where the top of the tent should be, and I went to Him through the air. When I reached Him, together we continued on to Heaven. We came to the Throne of God, and I beheld it in all its splendor.

I was not able to look upon the face of God; I only beheld His form.

The first thing that attracted my attention was the rainbow about the throne. It was so beautiful. The second thing I noticed was the winged creatures on either side of the throne. They were peculiar-looking creatures, and as I walked up with Jesus, these creatures stood with wings outstretched. They had been saying something, but when we approached, they ceased and folded their wings. They had eyes of fire set all around their heads, and they looked in all directions at once.

I stood with Jesus in the midst, about eighteen to twenty-four feet from the throne. I looked at the rainbow first, at the winged creatures, and then I started to look at the One who sat upon the throne. Jesus told me not to look upon His face. I could only see a form of a Being seated upon the throne.

Jesus talked to me for nearly an hour. I saw Him as plainly as I ever saw anyone in my life. I heard Him speak.

Looking into Love

And, for the first time, I actually looked into Jesus' eyes. Many times when relating this experience, I am asked, "What did His eyes look like?" All I can say is that they looked like wells of living love. It seemed as if one could see half a mile deep into them, and the tender look of His love is indescribable. As I looked into His face and into His eyes, I fell at His feet.

I noticed then that His feet were bare, and I laid the palms of my hands on the top of His feet and my forehead on the back of my hands. Weeping, I said, "O Lord, no one as unworthy as I should look upon your face!"

Jesus told me to stand upright on my feet. I stood up. He called me *worthy* to look upon His face, because He had called me and had cleansed me from all sin. He told me things concerning my ministry. He went on to say that He had called me before I was born. He said that although Satan had tried to destroy my life many times, His angels had watched over me and had cared for me.

Jesus told me that even as He had appeared to my mother before I was born and had told her, "Fear not, the child will be born," I would minister in the power of the Spirit and would fulfill the ministry He had called me to.

Then He talked to me about the last church I had pastored, saying that at that time, February 1949, I had entered into the first phase of my ministry. He said that some ministers he had called to the ministry live and die without getting into even the first phase He has for them. Jesus added that is one reason why many ministers die prematurely — they are living only in His permissive will!

God's Permissive Will

For fifteen years I had been only in His permissive will. I had been a pastor for twelve years and had been in evangelistic work for three. During those years God permitted me to do it, but it wasn't His perfect will for my life. And He said that, I hadn't been waiting on *Him*; *He* had been waiting for *me* to obey Him.

Then He talked about the time I entered into the *first* phase of my ministry in 1949. He said I had been unfaithful and hadn't done what He had told me to do; I hadn't told the people what He had told me to tell them. I answered, "Lord, I wasn't unfaithful. I *did* obey You. I left my church and went out in the evangelistic field."

"Yes," He said, "you left the church and went out in evangelistic work. But you didn't do what I told you to do. The reason you didn't is, you doubted it was my Spirit who had spoken to you. You see, faith obeys My Word, whether it is the written Word of God or by My Spirit who has spoken unto man."

I fell down before Him, saying, "Yes, Lord, I have failed, and I am sorry." I repented with many tears because I had missed His will and had doubted His dealings with me.

"Stand up on your feet," He said. As I stood before Him again, He told me that I had entered into the *second* phase of my ministry in January 1950, and at that time He had spoken to me by prophecy and by the still small voice in my heart. In the next eight months, during this second phase of my ministry, I had believed, I had been faithful, and I had obeyed.

Now I was to enter into the *third* phase, He said. If I would be faithful to what He told me — if I would believe and obey Him — He would appear to me again. At that time I would enter into the *fourth* and final stage of my ministry.

Seeing Jesus' Wounds

Then the Lord said to me, "Stretch forth thine hand!" He held His own hands out before Him, and I looked into them. For some reason I expected to see a scar in each hand where the nails had pierced His flesh. I should have known better, but many times we get ideas that are not really scriptural, yet they are accepted beliefs.

Instead of scars I saw in the palms of His hands the wounds of the crucifixion — three cornered, jagged holes. Each hole was big enough for me to have put my finger into it. I could see light on the other side of the hole.

After the vision, I got out my Bible and turned to the twentieth chapter in John's Gospel to read about the time Christ appeared to His disciples following His resurrection.

When He first appeared to them, Thomas was not with them. They told Thomas they had seen the Lord, but Thomas was unbelieving and said, ". . . *Except I shall see in his hands the print of the nails, and put my finger into the print of the nails, and thrust my hand into his side, I will not believe"* (John 20:25).

Eight days later while the disciples, including Thomas, were together in a room, Jesus appeared again in their midst. He turned to Thomas and said, *"Reach hither thy finger, and behold my hands; and reach hither thy hand, and thrust it into my side: and be not faithless, but believing."* Then Thomas, knowing it was Jesus, exclaimed, *"My Lord and my God"* (John 20:27,28).

I had deeper insight then into what Thomas had seen. He could have put His finger into the wound in Jesus' hand, and he could have thrust his hand into the Lord's side.

As I looked upon the wounds in His hands outstretched before me, I did as He instructed and held my hands out in front of me. He laid the finger of His right hand in the palm of my right hand and then in the palm of my left hand. The moment He did, my hands began to burn as if a coal of fire had been placed in them.

Jesus Gives Me a Special Anointing

Then Jesus told me to kneel down before Him. When I did, He laid His hand upon my head, saying that He had called me and had given me a special anointing to minister to the sick.

He went on to instruct me that when I pray and lay hands on the sick, I was to lay one hand on each side of the body. If I felt the fire jump from hand to hand, an evil spirit or demon was present in that body causing affliction. I should call him out in Jesus' Name, and the demon or demons would have to go.

If the fire, or the anointing, in my hands did not jump from hand to hand, it was a case of needing healing only. I should pray for the person in Jesus' Name, and if he would believe and accept it, the anointing would leave my hands and go into that person's body, driving out the disease and bringing healing. When the fire or anointing left my hands and went into the person's body, I would know he was healed.

I fell at Jesus' feet and pleaded, "Lord, don't send me. Send somebody else, Lord. *Please* don't send me. Just give me a little church to pastor somewhere. I would rather not go, Lord. I have heard so much criticism of those who pray for the sick. I just want a commonplace ministry."

Jesus rebuked me, saying, "I'll go with you and stand by your side as you pray for the sick, and many times you will see Me. Occasionally, I will open the eyes of someone in the audience and they will say, 'Why, I saw Jesus standing by that man as he prayed for the sick.'"

Jesus went on to ask who had called me: He or the people?

"Well, *You* did, Lord."

Don't Fear People

He explained that I should fear Him and not people, because even though people may criticize me, they are not my judge. I will stand before His judgment seat one day to give an account to Him for what I have done with my ministry, whether I have used it rightly or wrongly.

"All right, Lord, " I said. "I'll go if You'll go with me."

Then there swelled up in my heart a love such as I had never known for those who criticize this type of ministry. I said, "Lord, I'll pray for them, for they don't know, or they wouldn't say the things they do. Lord, I've said similar things, but I didn't realize or see as I do now, and neither do they. Forgive them, Lord."

Then He said, "Go thy way, my son; fulfill thy ministry and be thou faithful, for the time is short."

As I walked away from the Throne of God, Jesus told me, "Be sure to give Me all the praise and glory for all that is done, and be careful about money. Many of my servants whom I have anointed for this type of ministry have become money-minded and have lost the anointing and ministry I gave them.

"There are many who would pay much to be delivered. Many parents in the world have children whose little bodies are twisted, and they would give thousands of dollars for their healing. Many of them shall be delivered as you lay hands on them, but you must not accept a charge for your ministry. Accept offerings as you have been doing. You must go your way. Be faithful, for the time is short."

Jesus then journeyed with me back to the earth, and I realized that I still lay on my face on the floor. He talked to me there a moment and then disappeared. Then the vision ended.[1]

I was never the same after that experience. Over the years I have always tried to give God all the glory for anything that might have been accomplished through my efforts and to be extremely careful and aboveboard in every dealing that involved money. No amount of money is worth jeopardizing the anointing and calling of God in my life.

Does that mean that I was never to receive any financial reward for my labor? Absolutely not. In fact, the Lord told me to continue receiving offerings from people. But I understood that I was never to charge for my ministry — to make people feel obligated to pay me a specific amount for teaching or praying for them.

From the time I left the pastorate and went out on the field as an evangelist, I made it a personal policy to never take up an offering for myself. I asked the pastor of the church where I was ministering to simply tell the people, "This offering is for our evangelist, Brother Hagin."

Now I often would take up offerings during the meeting for the church or the pastor. Sometimes the offering would be for a special need or project for the church. Because I shared with them the scriptural principles of giving and prosperity, the people often responded more enthusiastically and generously than usual. Pastors would tell me that the offerings I took up were the largest they had ever received.

"Are you sure you don't want to take up your own offering, Brother Hagin?" they would ask. And I would always decline. I wanted my motives and priorities to be unmistakably clear. My primary purpose was to bless the people and the pastor — the church — not to benefit me personally. Yet the Lord always met my needs and provided a way for my family to prosper as well.

In all the years I ministered as a traveling evangelist in various churches across the country, I never took up an offering for myself. I bent over backwards to avoid even the slightest possibility of anyone thinking I was self-seeking. Like the Apostle

Paul wrote, I wanted to abstain from all appearance of evil (1 Thess. 5:22).

Don't misunderstand me. I am not suggesting that any evangelist who has ever taken his own offering in a church meeting is violating ministerial ethics or lacks personal integrity. I'm sure there are many fine men and women of God who have received offerings for their personal ministry whose motives were pure and who would never have violated the trust of the people.

But in my own case, I felt that the Lord had specifically directed me to be extra careful about money. So I tried to set a personal standard that never allowed me to be tempted and that could not be challenged by any reasonable person. I believe that it was the right thing for me and that God has honored my actions.

Later on when I started Kenneth Hagin Ministries, we often conducted independent crusades, seminars, conferences, and campmeetings outside of a local church. In these meetings, we did receive our own offerings, but they went to the organization, never to me personally.

When we have independent meetings, of course, Kenneth Hagin Ministries is responsible for all the costs and expenses. We pay the rent for the auditorium, the advertising, the motel and restaurant bills, travel costs, and all other expenses. Our ministry team members receive regular salaries paid from the ministry's income.

We have always let the people who attend our services know what their offerings are being used for. Once the budget for the meeting expenses is met, any additional funds received are channeled to one or more projects or outreaches of the ministry.

From the beginning, we set up our ministry to be financially accountable. We set up a non-profit corporation that was recognized and approved by our state government as well as the United States Internal Revenue Service. The ministry corporation has a board of advisors of respected businessmen who meet and review all financial transactions. Also, the ministry's financial records are audited by a national accounting firm that certifies their accuracy and compliance with all applicable state and national laws. We try our best to be good and faithful stewards of every dollar placed in our care.

Tithes Belong to the Local Church

Over the years, I have always championed the work and ministry of local churches and pastors. I believe the Church, which is the Body of Christ, is God's primary instrument to carry out His will and His work. This in no way lessens the value and need for missionaries, evangelists, and other para-church organizations. But the local church is the sheepfold — the place where individual believers are fed and strengthened, nurtured and cared for, trained and equipped. The local church is also the base for community ministry and various outreaches to the world.

As a general principle, I believe people should tithe to their local church. In so doing, they are supporting the ministers who care for them and their families. They are helping maintain a positive presence and witness in their community, and assisting the poor and needy, as well as providing support for missions and other outreaches.

Various other ministries can and should be supported by individuals and churches with offerings and other forms of financial support. These ministries and organizations perform a vital and wonderful service to the cause of Christ and are deserving of the prayers and financial gifts of their friends and supporters.

I have made it a point never to ask for the tithe from those who attend our services, tune in to our broadcasts, or read our publications. Instead, I encourage the friends of our ministry to pay their tithe to their local church and give any support they want us to have as an offering. I believe this is the biblical pattern and the proper way to seek support.

There have been a few cases in which people have said they felt they should tithe to our ministry because we provided their sole spiritual nurture. Perhaps there wasn't a church near them, and they weren't able to get out of the house. Our radio and television programs, our tapes, books, videos, and other materials provided their spiritual food and care. In those unusual circumstances, we prayerfully accepted their tithe. But in the overwhelming majority of cases, we urge folks to tithe to their local churches.

Forsake Not the Assembling Of Yourselves Together

The Word directs us to come together with other believers to worship God, to encourage each other, and to receive instruction and inspiration. Church is the best place I know of for that to happen.

Hebrews 10:25 says, *"Not forsaking the assembling of ourselves together, as the manner of some is; but exhorting one another: and so much the more, as ye see the day approaching."* I've never found any scriptures that make exceptions to this. Watching Christian TV, listening to ministry programs on the radio, listening to teaching tapes, watching videos, and reading Christian books are fine and good, and I believe in them. But they don't take the place of the local church.

I know there are people who say they don't go to church anymore because television is their pastor. "I like watching Brother Smith," they say. "He's like my pastor."

But Brother Smith can't be their pastor because he's *not* a pastor; he doesn't minister in that office. Unless he has a church, he's not a pastor.

Some years ago, I heard a popular evangelist make a statement to a small group of ministers in a private setting that was appalling to me. He said, "Well, I don't much believe in the local church. If people hear my broadcast, listen to my tapes, and read my books, they can stay at home and be just as good a Christian as they would if they went to church."

I commented to a couple of the ministers who heard him, "Isn't it a shame that poor old Jesus wasn't as smart as him? Evidently, poor old God didn't know that. He sent pastors to be shepherds and wrote in His Word for us not to forsake the assembling of ourselves together!"

As soon as I had the opportunity, I asked this man, "Are you a shepherd — a pastor?"

"Oh, no, no," he replied. "That's not my calling."

"Then how could anybody be a successful Christian by just listening to your tapes and reading your books?" I asked him. He didn't seem to have a good answer to my question.

God uses the church to minister and meet the everyday needs of His people. The church is a family, and we all need the support of a family. We understand how a regular family cares for a new baby, feeding and tending to all its needs as it grows. After a while, the family helps the little one learn to walk, start taking care of itself, and then begin to do simple tasks and chores. Eventually, the child learns how to contribute to the family and become a productive member of society.

The church family performs a similar function for new Christians. After a time of concentrated care and training, young Christians are taught how to worship God and are given the opportunity to begin serving the Lord. They may start out with simple things such as learning the Bible and how to worship and pray. Then they begin using their talents to bless and help others. Whatever their abilities, they soon find something they can do to contribute to and be part of God's work.

Only a church family can provide this kind of support and involvement. You can't get this experience through tapes or books. Christian radio and television tends to make people spectators who are simply sitting on the sidelines watching or listening. Gospel broadcasts and other materials often have excellent spiritual content that is entertaining and edifying; they have a valid place in the Kingdom of God. But they can't replace the function of the local church in training and equipping people for Christian service.

Who Will Be There for You in the Crises of Life?

Sooner or later, all of us experience some of the crises of life, and it's important to have somewhere to turn and to have caring people sustain us.

For example, what would you do if you were depending on a TV program to be your pastor and you ended up in the hospital with a serious illness? Who would come to pray for you and encourage you to trust in God?

What if one of your loved ones passed away? Could you call that TV preacher to come comfort you, help you make the final arrangements, and conduct the funeral? Would anyone prepare food and bring it to your house for those who were grieving with you?

What if your son or daughter wanted to get married? Who would provide the premarital counseling, minister to the wedding party, and perform the marriage ceremony? Would you be able to depend on your radio pastor or TV church to meet your needs?

Don't you count on it!

There are times when you want and need the presence and touch of real, live, flesh-and-blood people you can trust. You need the support and help of people who know and love you — family members.

Acts chapter 4 tells about an incident in the life of Peter and John that illustrates what I'm talking about. After speaking healing to a crippled beggar outside the temple in Jerusalem and preaching Jesus to the crowd that had gathered, Peter and John were arrested by the religious leaders and put in jail overnight. After being questioned and threatened, they finally were released.

What do you do when you've tried to help others and take a stand for the Lord only to be persecuted for your efforts? Where do you go when you've been put in jail overnight and then dumped out on the street? What did Peter and John do?

The Bible says, "*And being let go, they went to their own company . . .*" (Acts 4:23). They knew where to go when they got in trouble. They didn't go listen to tapes or read a book. They didn't listen to Brother Smith's radio broadcast or watch his TV program. They went to find the people who knew and loved them — fellow believers who shared their faith.

I believe Peter and John's "company" of friends gave them a place to take a bath and clean up and provided them with some clean clothes. Then they fixed them something to eat and listened while Peter and John told what had happened to them. Afterwards, they all prayed together until the Holy Ghost fell and shook the house. Then they continued to speak the Word of God with boldness (*see* Acts 4:31).

We all need our own company of believers, don't we? If we just stay home and listen to someone preach on radio or TV, we don't have any company! We need a place to go where we can find people of God. We need to meet together to support and help each other and to mobilize our resources to do God's work and carry out the Great Commission. That's why God tells us not to forsake the assembling of ourselves together in the local church (Heb. 10:25).

That's why it's more important to support your local church financially than to give anywhere else. Pay your tithes to your local church to help it carry out all its work and outreaches. Yes, there are other worthy ministries that are also deserving of your support. Don't leave them out; send offerings to assist their work as God blesses you and makes it possible for you to share.

As you follow this pattern, I believe God will use you to help bless your church and pastoral staff and to prosper other good men and women of God who are accomplishing great things for the Lord. And I also believe that God will meet all your needs and abundantly bless you — spiritually, physically, and materially. Only then will you experience the true meaning of prosperity.

---

[1]For a more detailed account of these visions, *see* Rev. Hagin's book *I Believe in Visions*.

CHAPTER SIX

AVOIDING ABUSES AND FALSE PRACTICES

Money is a necessary commodity in today's civilization. For the overwhelming majority of people, the days in which the members of a family worked together to be largely self-sufficient — building their own house, growing their own food, providing their own water and fuel, creating their own clothing, and using "natural" means of transportation — is a distant memory.

Today all the products and services needed for even an ordinary lifestyle must be purchased. Going through a single day without spending money for something is difficult, if not impossible. Just as this dependence on money affects the way most people live their day-to-day lives, it also has a major impact on the way churches and ministries carry out their work.

Finding Money for Ministry

Fundraising has become a fact of life — a necessary part of every effective Christian organization if it is to survive.

Gordon Lindsay was one of the leading ministers of the Pentecostal movement and the healing revival in the twentieth century. He was also the founder of the ministry organization now known as Christ for the Nations. A prolific writer and publisher, Rev. Lindsay often spoke out about the perils and problems ministers face in finding money for ministry. Some of his comments are included in an earlier chapter. In his book *The Charismatic Ministry*, he wrote the following:

[Money] is an important element in promoting Christian work. Its availability to a considerable extent governs the scope of our activities. It is, therefore, natural that a minister looks for ways and means by which he can secure necessary funds for the work that he feels called to do.

But here lurks many pitfalls in which the unwary may stumble. The line between the permissible and the objectionable is sometimes very thin. Some men have raised hundreds of thousands of dollars for missions, and their work is to be highly praised. Others have raised comparatively insignificant amounts, and the manner in which it was done or the way they used it, has called forth strong condemnation.

If people are told that the money is to be used for a certain purpose, and it is spent largely for other things, such as for promotion, then it is being raised under false pretenses. This is a sore point. Certainly there are costs in raising missionary money. Anyone who says otherwise doesn't speak the truth. But if the greater proportion of the funds so raised are used for overhead, then something is wrong. . . .

The manner of taking offerings in a campaign is extremely important. If every service or a considerable number of services is occupied with a lengthy appeal for large offerings, the effect upon the people of the community is likely to be unfavorable. The ministers so engaged will soon be regarded as employed mainly in money raising.[1]

Lindsay also commented on the use of "gimmicks" he had seen over the years that were used by various religious groups as a means of fundraising. He stated the following:

Gimmicks which included relics, bones, holy water, indulgences, etc., cursed the Medieval Church. They were widely used at that time as money-raising devices designed to appeal to people's ignorance and superstition. Today certain preachers are resorting to gimmicks to entice people to part with their money. . . .

What we are referring to as gimmicks is the use of articles that purport to have some mysterious power or supposed virtue in them — a sort of charm or fetish — the use of which has no Scriptural foundation. . . .

What are some of these gimmicks? The number apparently is endless, for new ones are heard of frequently. The partial list includes such things as follows: a "blessed purse" that causes money to multiply "supernaturally"; the "gift" of prosperity; "magic pictures" in which the image reappears after the person has closed his eyes . . . ; a special "prayer carpet"; "holy oil" or "holy water" that is supposed to carry a special virtue; cloths which "supernaturally" change color; "blessed nails"; "blessed pictures"; "blessed sawdust" on which an angel is supposed to have walked; a barrel of water in which an angel comes down and "troubles it"; "bottled demons," etc. These are only a few of the long list of gimmicks which have been offered to the public.

The Reformation actually had its beginning when Martin Luther became convinced that all the gimmicks the church used — the relics, the saints' bones, splinters from the "true cross," etc. — were phony and had no virtue. May God help the minister to abide in the simplicity and purity of the gospel and not attempt to mislead people with such things.[2]

Lindsay was also quoted by the respected author, David Edwin Harrell, Jr., in his study of the Pentecostal movement, *All Things Are Possible*. Noting the concern of responsible leaders of the healing revival over the "improper emphasis on money," the book recorded Lindsay's warning against a covetous spirit.

> But this revival can be greatly retarded if there is a continual auctioneering for money in the campaigns. There are some who are short-sighted enough to have destroyed their usefulness to the kingdom of God by an offensive handling of finances.[3]

Harrell also quoted Donald Gee, who, as we noted earlier, was an influential British Christian editor who came to believe that the healing movement had harbored frauds and promoted exploitation. He declared, "It has to be confessed that in a few regrettable cases commercialism vitiated [debased] the testimony."[4]

In his own book *A Way To Escape*, Gee said, "Good and faithful preaching of the full gospel has been weakened by unscriptural appeals for money, to the stumbling of many."[5]

The warnings of these and other Christian leaders need to be heard and heeded again by every honest minister and

Christian organization today. Unfortunately, the same kinds of abuses and mistaken practices involving money that have plagued the Church since the days of the Apostles are still flourishing today.

No minister is immune to temptations regarding money. The devil is sure to come around when there are opportunities to compromise scriptural standards and our personal principles of financial integrity. It would be easy to rationalize and make excuses for improperly seeking support when we're under financial pressure or when an admiring crowd could easily be influenced into giving a substantial personal "love offering."

The spiritual dangers of giving in to this kind of temptation are tremendous. The Bible issues a stern warning that could apply in such a situation: "*Wherefore let him that thinketh he standeth take heed lest he fall*" (1 Cor. 10:12).

There are a number of teachings and practices in the Church today, particularly among Charismatic groups, that can lead to misunderstandings and hurtful problems. Many times, these errors are the result of people taking a Bible verse, or part of a verse, out of context or by carrying an application too far. Sometimes there has been an overzealous attempt to make a New Testament application of some Old Testament phrase or technicality that absolutely does not apply. Taken to the extreme, these teachings can become abuses and false practices.

Let's examine several specific examples that are being taught in various places across this country and in some other nations as well. While there may not be any malicious intent on the part of those who have promoted these teachings, I believe these teachings have the potential to injure and victimize innocent people.

Is Financial Prosperity a Sign of Spirituality?

One teaching supposes that financial prosperity is a sure sign of spirituality. This teaching suggests that throughout the Bible, God has rewarded faith and holiness with material blessings. The implication is that if a person is not experiencing financial abundance, there must be a spiritual deficit in his life — probably caused by not giving enough.

For example, the teacher might quote Matthew 6:33 and say, "If you're not having 'all these things' added to your life, you must not be seeking first the Kingdom of God." This is the same kind of abuse as telling a person who has not received healing for a sickness or disease that evidently he just doesn't have enough faith.

The truth is that receiving a financial windfall is not a sure and absolute indicator of the blessings of God. It could also be an indicator that the person robbed a bank or "got lucky" gambling in Las Vegas! If wealth alone were a sign of spirituality, then drug traffickers and crime bosses would be spiritual giants. The Bible says that those who suppose that gain is godliness are "men of corrupt minds," filled with perverse disputings and destitute of the truth (*see* First Timothy 6:5).

While several scriptures do link material prosperity with the blessings of God, numerous other verses make a sharp distinction and differentiation between material wealth and spiritual blessings.

Proverbs 10:22 says, *"The blessing of the Lord, it maketh rich, and he addeth no sorrow with it."* But the Apostle James writes, *"Let the brother of low degree rejoice in that he is exalted: But the rich, in that he is made low: because as the flower of the grass he shall pass away . . . Hearken, my beloved brethren, Hath not God chosen the poor of this world rich in faith, and heirs of the kingdom which he hath promised to them that love him?"* (James 1:9,10; 2:5).

In Paul's first letter to Timothy, he gives him some advice. *But godliness with contentment is great gain. For we brought nothing into this world, and it is certain we can carry nothing out. And having food and raiment let us be therewith content. But they that will be rich fall into temptation and a snare, and into many foolish and hurtful lusts, which drown men in destruction and perdition . . . Charge them that are rich in this world, that they be not*

highminded, nor trust in uncertain riches, but in the living
God, who giveth us richly all things to enjoy.

— 1 Timothy 6:6-9,17

Several verses in the Book of Proverbs indicate that there are some types of blessings that are more beneficial and desirable than material blessings, if and when such a choice were ever necessary.

Better is little with the fear of the Lord than great treasure and trouble therewith.

— Proverbs 15:16

Better is a little with righteousness than great revenues without right.

— Proverbs 16:8

Better is the poor that walketh in his uprightness, than he that is perverse in his ways, though he be rich.

— Proverbs 28:6

In short, material wealth can be connected to the blessings of God or it can be totally *disconnected* from the blessings of God. Certainly, financial prosperity is not an infallible gauge of a person's spirituality.

Giving To Get

A popular teaching in recent years has been that giving should be mechanically linked to getting. If you need something, give something. Sow a car to get a car. Sow a suit to receive a suit.

This is another example of taking a basic truth and carrying it to the extreme. Like any other biblical truth, there is a ditch of error on both sides of the road.

There are some people who do not seem to realize that God wants to bless them. They have no understanding at all of the practical application of the law of sowing and reaping in their personal lives. As a result, giving for them is strictly a matter of duty. They may give, but they have no faith or expectation whatsoever about receiving anything from God. This is unfortunate because they undoubtedly miss out on some of the blessings that God has for them.

On the other side of the road are the greedy folks who are attempting to use their giving to manipulate God. They try to make the offering plate some kind of heavenly vending machine — put in your offering, pull the handle, and get your blessing back! This is certainly the wrong motive for giving.

Some people go so far with this kind of thinking that they get into foolishness, giving away their car in the hope of getting another, presumably better, car. These people sometimes end up walking for a long time!

I am quite sure that there could be an occasion when God would deal with an individual about giving his car to some person or ministry. If that person then gave away his car out of obedience and love, as unto the Lord, I believe God would bless him in return, perhaps with another vehicle. But God's specific, personal direction for one individual does not become an across-the-board doctrine for the whole Church. There is no spiritual formula to sow a Ford and reap a Mercedes.

Many preachers have used the story of the widow of Zarephath as an example of a person giving out of her need and being prospered in return. According to First Kings 17, there was a famine in the land, and this poor widow was down to her last handful of flour and few drops of oil. She was about to prepare one last meal for herself and her son and then starve to death.

Elijah, the prophet, asked her to prepare a cake of bread for him first and then cook for herself and her son. He told her that the Lord said, "The jar of flour will not be used up and the jug of oil will not run dry until the day the Lord gives rain on the land" (see First Kings 17:14 NIV). When she obeyed by giving bread to Elijah, her supply was miraculously multiplied; she received bread.

Jesus referred specifically to this event in the very beginning of His earthly ministry. He said, "I assure you that there were many widows in Israel in Elijah's time, when the sky was shut for three and a half years and there was a severe famine throughout the land. Yet Elijah was not sent to any of them, but to a widow in Zarephath in the region of Sidon. And there were many in Israel with leprosy in the time of Elisha the prophet, yet not one of them was cleansed — only Naaman the Syrian" (Luke 4:25-27 *NIV*).

The Bible clearly teaches that God is no respecter of persons (Acts 10:34). His love and blessings are available to all. But there is no absolute spiritual law that says every individual will experience the love and blessings of God in exactly the same way.

I believe that healing is for all. But Jesus declared that not all people will be healed in the way that Naaman the leper was. I believe that prosperity is for all, but Jesus said that not all people are going to be prospered the way the widow of Zarephath was. God did not tell every sick person to dip seven times in the Jordan River, and He didn't tell every needy person to give their last bit of food to Elijah. There are no one-size-fits-all rules for healing and prosperity.

If the Lord speaks to you in a clear and compelling way to give your coat to someone, then do it. But give it out of love and obedience to God. In that case, I believe God will reward you and not leave you shivering in your shirt sleeves. But be sure of your motives in giving your coat. Don't do it just because you heard the testimony of some other person who gave away a coat and was blessed with a new leather jacket. Don't say, "I want a leather jacket, too, so I'll give away my coat."

Our motives are crucially important. We need to be willing to give in obedience to God even if we never receive one thing in return. We must keep our hearts right and guard against covetousness. At the same time, we need to realize that God does want us to have faith, expecting Him to meet our needs.

Naming Your Seed

Some ministers have put a great deal of emphasis on the practice of "naming your seed." They have told people, "When you get your offering out, give it a name. If a farmer wants to harvest corn, he plants corn. If he wants to harvest cotton, he plants cotton. So name your offering as seed for what you want to receive."

I'm not sure that "naming your seed" is necessarily scriptural. I can't find any verses that specifically support the practice. Perhaps for some people it is a way of being specific about what they are believing God for. It is good to be specific with our faith, but I also believe it's important not to try to restrict the benefits of a particular offering to a specific result.

I am not saying that sowing seed is wrong; I am simply addressing the practice of *naming* your seed. The Bible plainly points out that God intends for us to sow and reap, and that includes sowing and reaping in the area of finances.

The Bible teaches that God will bless His children when they are walking according to His Word (Deut. 28). I believe the primary means whereby God will bless you is through the law of sowing and reaping. In other words, when you are faithful to simply give your tithe and offerings, God is faithful to ". . . *open you the windows of heaven, and pour you out a blessing, that there shall not be room enough to receive it*" (Mal. 3:10).

As I stated in a previous chapter, the tithe is ten percent of your income. Offerings are whatever amount you purpose in your heart to give, or what the Holy Spirit leads you to give, *over and above* the tithe. Tithes and offerings are the primary pattern of giving and receiving that God has ordained for the prospering of His children.

I personally don't "name my seed," saying that I'm giving my offering in order to reap such-and-such. I just believe God to supply all my needs. I believe that the Lord is my Shepherd and that I shall not want. So I give because I love the Lord.

Because "naming your seed" is not a Bible-based practice, I would urge preachers to be careful not to use this as a gimmick to persuade people to give.

A fellow minister once said, "Being focused on what we receive as a result of our giving corrupts the very attitude of our giving nature. Our focus must not be on what we receive as the result. Rather, our focus needs to be on giving as an expression of our love for our Lord and Savior and the fact that it pleases Him."

For several years, I have conducted All Faiths' Crusades in churches and auditoriums across the country. I have made it a practice to present the work of RHEMA Bible Training Center at some time during the crusade and to use the proceeds or offerings from the meeting for the school. These funds have helped keep the doors of the school open, since the tuition received from students only pays for about a third of the actual operating costs.

But raising funds for RHEMA is not my sole purpose in conducting crusades — nor is it even my first priority. Although it is a worthy cause that is deserving of support, I do not invest my time and effort just to get an offering for the school.

I have a list of purposes, arranged by priorities:

1. To get people born again

2. To get people filled with the Holy Spirit

3. To get people healed

4. To help establish believers in faith

5. To present RHEMA Bible Training Center for financial support

I believe every believer should have a similar prioritized list of purposes for giving; such a list might look like this:

1. Because I love God
2. Because I want to obey God
3. Because I want to support the Great Commission and the Church
4. Because I want to see people blessed
5. Because I am planting seed for my own needs

The Hundredfold Return

The idea that God will reward our giving by paying a one-hundred-to-one return on what we give to His work has become a very popular concept. It is almost commonplace to hear ministers refer to it at offering time, urging people to "give generously and believe God for a hundredfold blessing."

The basis for this concept is a passage of Scripture included in the Gospels of Matthew, Mark, and Luke.

Then Peter began to say unto him, Lo, we have left all, and have followed thee. And Jesus answered and said, Verily I say unto you, There is no man that hath left house, or brethren, or sisters, or father, or mother, or wife, or children, or lands, for my sake, and the gospel's, but he shall receive an HUNDREDFOLD now in this time, houses, and brethren, and sisters, and mothers,

and children, and lands, with persecutions; and in the
world to come eternal life.

— Mark 10:28-30

Notice that there is nothing said in this passage about tithes or offerings. The context refers to people who have made an absolute commitment to follow the call of God upon their lives, leaving their former possessions, families, and lifestyles behind (*see* also Matthew 19:27-29 and Luke 18:28-30).

Jesus responded to Peter by saying, "Every man who sacrifices his all for My sake, and the Gospel's, shall receive a hundredfold in this life of houses, brothers, sisters, fathers, mothers, children, lands, and persecutions" (Mark 10:29,30).

What did Jesus mean? Was He literally promising each disciple a hundred pieces of real estate for each one they had forsaken, and a hundred brothers or sisters for each sibling left at home, and a hundred fathers, mothers, or children? In studying the lives of the disciples, we find no record of any of them ever acquiring such possessions — except for persecutions.

Did Jesus' words fail to come true? Was He exaggerating? I don't think so. There is no account of any disciple ever complaining about the Lord's broken promises. Instead, they testified that His record was true!

What did Jesus mean when He said they would receive a hundredfold of houses and family? Wiser men than me who have spent lifetimes studying the Scriptures and the life and times of Jesus have given their interpretation. To these itinerant evangelists who would become missionaries to the world, traveling alone with little more than the clothes on their backs, He promised that houses in strange lands would open their doors to them — a hundred, if need be. He promised that as they preached the Gospel of the Kingdom and won souls to Christ, they would enjoy fellowship with countless brothers, sisters, mothers, and fathers — a multiplied family of faith.

Is the hundredfold return available for us today? Yes, of course, it's available for all who have left everything to commit their all for the sake of Christ and the Gospel!

Does the hundredfold return mean that when we give an offering, we should get out a calculator and compute the monetary payback we expect to receive at the rate of one hundred to one? In other words, if we give a dollar to God's work, are we promised that He will give us a hundred dollars back?

Let's consider a hypothetical example of what would happen if an individual actually had this happen just seven times in his life. Since the purpose of prosperity is to provide believers with the resources to do God's work, we'll assume that once this individual began his giving with a dollar and received his multiplied return, he "reinvested" the total amount back into the Kingdom of God by giving again.

Here's how that scenario would play out with the hundredfold return working a mere seven times:

$1 x hundredfold return = $100

$100 x hundredfold return = $10,000

$10,000 x hundredfold return = $1,000,000

(*Note:* If the hundredfold return worked just three times from an initial dollar offering, the donor would be a millionaire!)

$1,000,000 x hundredfold return = $100,000,000

(That's a hundred million dollars!)

$100,000,000 x hundredfold return = $10,000,000,000

   (ten billion dollars)

$10,000,000,000 x hundredfold return =

   $1,000,000,000,000 (one trillion dollars)

$1,000,000,000,000 x hundredfold return =

   $100,000,000,000,000 (one hundred trillion dollars!)

At the time of this writing, the man with the most financial wealth in the world is considered to be Bill Gates of Microsoft; his net worth is estimated to be as much as $85 billion. So a person for whom the hundredfold return worked as described above would have 1,176 times more money than Bill Gates!

Perhaps you know of a Christian who has been very generous in his giving and has strong faith in God's ability and willingness to give prosperity to His children. Let's say that over the years this person accumulates a net worth of ten million dollars. Most people would agree that this individual is quite wealthy — that financial prosperity is a reality to him.

However, this wealthy Christian's ten million dollars is a microscopic fraction of what could be realized on the hundredfold return on an initial dollar offering reinvested seven times as described above. In fact, that ten million dollars would have to be multiplied ten million times to equal the hundred trillion dollars hypothetically received by the individual who had his single dollar returned a hundredfold just seven times over.

Consider also that almost any Christian who is faithful in tithes and offerings would not have begun with a single dollar, but hundreds of dollars! If the hundredfold return worked literally and mathematically for everyone who gave money in an offering, we would have Christians walking around with not billions or trillions of dollars, but quadrillions of dollars!

Interpret the Word of God Correctly

Please understand that I am not trying to be cynical, nor am I trying to take away anyone's faith concerning God meeting his needs. But I believe it is important that we be realistic and sound in what we teach. We must "rightly divide" the Word of God and carefully seek the truth in interpreting the Scriptures.

Overemphasizing or adding to what the Bible actually teaches invariably does more harm than good. Over the years, I have seen believers leap to false and totally unrealistic conclusions regarding teachings such as the hundredfold return. Feeling that they have been promised remarkable, extraordinary, and phenomenal returns, some have ended up disappointed and disillusioned when the result didn't materialize as they envisioned.

Going back to the original question — should a believer expect a monetary payback at the rate of one hundred to one when he pays his tithes or gives an offering? Absolutely not!

Then why do some preachers teach that? Well, ministers are just human, like everyone else. Sometimes we make mistakes. Every now and then, an idea or concept comes along that sounds really exciting; people are really taken with it and eager to respond to it. It's easy to just jump on the bandwagon and go along with the crowd without taking the time to search out the Scriptures and examine the idea in detail.

Several years ago, I made that mistake with the concept of the hundredfold return. I picked up on what others were saying and started saying it too. When I took an offering, I would pray that God would bless the people's giving by sending them a hundredfold return. It sounded good. And people seemed excited and enthusiastic about it. But every time I said it, I felt vaguely uncomfortable. Something wasn't quite right, but I couldn't put my finger on it.

One morning I was getting up to come teach a class at RHEMA. I was sitting on the side of the bed putting on my socks. I had one on and was starting to put the other one on when the Lord said to me, "No one has ever received a hundredfold return yet on all their giving."

Well, that stopped me in my tracks — with one sock on and one sock off. I thought, *Did I hear right? I believe I know the voice of the Lord. I've heard it many times.*

"Well, Lord," I said, "Jesus talked about the sower who went out and scattered seed. Not all of it produced good results, but some produced a hundredfold, some sixtyfold, and some thirty."

The Lord pointed out to me that the parable I was referring to was not talking about money. The seed is the Word. The stony and thorn-infested ground has no return at all — some who hear the Word do not respond. But even in good ground, the amount of return differs. Some Christians don't grow and develop much — maybe thirtyfold. Others may develop more. And some become great, devout, faith-filled, productive Christians — the hundredfold folks. In other words, they receive the maximum benefit from the Word of God they have heard.

And the other commonly used hundredfold passage that we looked at earlier isn't about giving money, either. Mark 10:28 through 30 is talking about Christian service. Jesus wasn't talking about multiplying tithes and offerings.

I believe it is quite possible that there may be some individuals who have given a certain amount and received a multiplied return on it, perhaps even a hundredfold — but not on *every* dollar they have ever given to the Lord! God's word to me was that no one has ever yet received a hundredfold return on *all* their giving. Have you?

If your tithes and offerings last year were $5,000, did you receive a hundredfold return of a half million dollars? If you gave a total of $20,000, did you receive $2,000,000? Do you expect to?

I think you get the point. I did, too, and that's why I no longer tell people to expect the hundredfold return on their offerings. I just stay with what the Word of God says: "*Give, and it shall be given unto you; good measure, pressed down, and shaken together, and running over . . .*" (Luke 6:38). I always claim the "running over" blessing.

A 'Debt-Breaking' or
'Money-Multiplying' Anointing

From time to time, people ask me about some preacher who either claims — or is said by others — to be especially anointed to "break the power of debt" over people's lives or to be able to "multiply people's money back to them." In most cases, this special anointing or ability can only be activated by giving an offering to this minister or the organization he represents.

There is not one bit of Scripture I know about that validates such a practice. I'm afraid that it is simply a scheme to raise money for the preacher, and ultimately it can turn out to be dangerous and destructive for all involved. We need to be extremely careful about elevating certain ministers to higher-than-human status. Our focus should be on God rather than man.

Certainly, money can be more productive for the Kingdom of God when it is sown into a productive ministry. And there are gifted ministers skilled at building confidence and motivating people. But Christians should be giving to help get the Gospel out and to do God's work, not to get some "highly anointed minister" to multiply their money back to them.

I'm reminded of Paul and Barnabas. When they ministered in the city of Lystra, a lifelong cripple was raised up, leaping and walking. When the people of the city saw what had happened, they cried, "The gods are come down to us in the likeness of men." They called Barnabas *Jupiter*, and called Paul *Mercurius*. The Bible says the priests of the city brought oxen and garlands to offer a sacrifice to them (*see* Acts 14:8-18).

In order to restrain the people from worshipping them, Paul and Barnabas had to run among the people and testify that they were just men in the service of the Living God. It seems there is something about human nature that wants to elevate certain people to god-like status.

The Greeks had a mythical legend about a king named Midas who lived in the eighth century B.C., from the same general area as Lystra. You probably remember his story as the king with the golden touch; everything he put his hands on turned to gold.

Well, just as the people of Lystra asked if Jupiter and Mercurius had come down amongst them, today it seems some people are asking, "Is Midas in our midst?"

Unfortunately, too many are ready to believe that if they put money into the hands of a preacher with the Midas touch, so to speak, he will somehow, magically, bring increase and multiplication of their finances. This can quickly degenerate into wrong motives or covetousness.

Some people may be tempted to give, not just to bless God's work, but out of greed for the material gain they hope to get for their own selfish purposes.

A person who feels that he is in bondage to debt may give a minister most or all of the money he has out of desperation. He hopes against hope that the minister will help him get such a miraculous return from his offering that he can pay off his debts and get a fresh start.

I've heard of people with large credit-card debts or medical bills who had been told to expect "supernatural debt cancellation." Then, through a computer mistake or human error, they received a statement showing that they no longer owed anything or owed a substantially smaller amount. In some cases, a bank deposit was posted incorrectly, giving them credit for a larger amount that was enough to pay off an indebtedness.

There is nothing "supernatural" about these kinds of events. Trying to take advantage of them will only lead to more trouble. If some kind of mistake is made in which a Christian is credited with money that he knows doesn't belong to him, he has a moral, ethical, and biblical obligation to rectify the matter.

It's been said that as a young man, Abraham Lincoln worked as a clerk in a store. A woman came in one day and purchased some items. Lincoln added up her bill, and it came to two dollars and six and a quarter cents. She paid the bill, was entirely satisfied, and left. Later, Lincoln began to question his calculation. He refigured it and realized the bill should have been two dollars even. That night when he locked the store, he walked two to three miles to her home and paid her the six and a quarter cents.

The Bible says, "If you see your brother's ox or sheep straying, do not ignore it but be sure to take it back to him. If the brother does not live near you or if you do not know who he is, take it home with you and keep it until he comes looking for it. Then give it back to him. Do the same if you find your brother's donkey or his cloak or anything he loses. Do not ignore it" (Deut. 22:1-3 NIV).

For most people, getting out of debt is not an instantaneous or overnight process. They don't experience a single miraculous "breakthrough" in which God dumps a big lump sum in their lap. Usually it involves many months — maybe years — of hard work, diligence, good money management, wisdom, living within one's means, and the blessings of God that come through faith.

The minister who claims to have a "debt-breaking" or "money-multiplying" anointing is in danger of being led deeper into error. Instead of presenting a balanced message of the full Gospel and fulfilling the call of God on his life, he may become a narrowly-focused "specialist," dealing only with money and financial gain. He may even develop into such a skilled fundraiser that he becomes a "hired gun," brought in by other ministry organizations to raise money for them (for a "cut" of the "take").

Instead of living to bless people, strengthen local churches, and advance the cause of Christ, such a preacher runs a great risk and faces great temptation of focusing only on what he can get for himself and his purposes. Somewhere along the way, his original call and mission gets laid aside. The Apostle Paul said, *"But I keep under my body, and bring it into subjection: lest that by any means, when I have preached to others, I myself should be a castaway"* (1 Cor. 9:27). That is much too high a price to pay for money.

Is Giving to the Poor a Good Investment?

It grieves my spirit to hear that there are some ministers teaching — or at least giving the impression — that giving to them *personally* will bring a greater blessing to the donor than giving to the poor or supporting the local church's ministry to the poor. Again, these individuals imply that because they have a "special anointing" like Jesus, they have a gift — a Midas touch — to multiply money back to the donor and impart great blessings.

Some of these ministers actually suggest that there is not much blessing in giving to the poor by quoting Proverbs 19:17: *"He that hath pity upon the poor lendeth unto the Lord; and that which he hath given will he pay him again."* "That's not too good an investment," they say. "Giving five dollars to a poor person is a loan to God, and He will pay you back five dollars. You get back just what you 'loaned' to God. But if you invest that five dollars in a ministry with a 'higher anointing,' you can expect a *multiplied* return."

Then they will say, "You know, Jesus said you will always have the poor with you . . ." (John 12:8) implying that the poor aren't worth much, that they're a dime a dozen.

This teaching is totally wrong and thoroughly unscriptural. Such suggestions are completely false interpretations of Proverbs 19:7 and John 12:8.

The idea that "loaning" a dollar to God by giving it to the poor will only bring a repayment of a dollar is not consistent with other Bible examples. John 5 tells how Jesus "borrowed" Peter's boat. He got into the boat and asked "the big fisherman" to put out from the shore a ways so He would have a platform to teach the crowd of people who had thronged about Him. Then Jesus repaid Peter for the loan of his boat.

Let's look at the following account in the Gospel of Luke.

When he had finished speaking, he said to Simon, "Put out into deep water, and let down the nets for a catch." Simon answered, "Master, we've worked hard all night and haven't caught anything. But because you say so, I will let down the nets." When they had done so, they caught such a large number of fish that their nets began to break. So they signaled their partners in the other boat to come and help them, and they came and filled both boats so full that they began to sink.

— Luke 5:4-7 (NIV)

How much was the use of Peter's fishing boat for an hour or so worth? It wasn't worth nearly as much as two overflowing boatloads of fish! Without question, Jesus repaid the loan with interest! He certainly wasn't a scrooge.

In the very next chapter of John's Gospel, we find the account of the feeding of the five thousand. You know the story: A little boy gave his lunch of five small barley loaves and two fish to Jesus, who multiplied them to feed the multitude of hungry people. When everyone had eaten, the disciples gathered up the leftovers — twelve baskets full! (*see* John 6:8-12.)

I'm of the opinion that Jesus gave those twelve baskets of bread and fish to that little boy who had given his lunch to the poor, "loaning" it to God. Several people must have had to help him carry all that food back home. He was repaid for his loan with bountiful interest.

You see, people often quote just one verse of Scripture on a subject that seems to give a certain impression, but they ignore many others. You can't build a doctrine on any one scripture. The Bible says, "*In the mouth of two or three witnesses shall every word be established*" (2 Cor. 13:1).

The Bible has much to say about helping and ministering to the poor. Let's start with the verse some ministers misuse. In John 12:8, Jesus says, "You will always have the poor among you." What Jesus really meant is disclosed in the Old Testament verse He was quoting: "There will always be poor people in the land. Therefore I command you to be open-handed toward your brothers and toward the poor and needy in your land" (Deut. 15:11 *NIV*).

So what Jesus was really saying, in essence, was this: "There will always be poor people to help, and you should help them as much as you can. You'll always have opportunities to help the poor, but I'll only be here a very short time."

Firstfruits

Many years ago, there was a teaching on firstfruits, which went back to the Old Covenant under the Levitical Law. It focused on the fact that the firstfruits were brought to the priests personally, and that these Old Covenant priests represented a type of present-day fivefold ministers because they were anointed. A serious problem develops when we begin referring to fivefold ministers as priests.

Remember, we mentioned earlier in this chapter that we don't pay tithes and give offerings in the same way they did under the Old Covenant. Under the Levitical Law, the people brought their firstfruits to the priest. But under the New Covenant, we have one High Priest — the Lord Jesus Christ.

Someone might ask, "What about the fivefold ministry? Aren't they priests? Don't those in fivefold ministry represent me to God?" No, they're not priests. They don't represent you to God; they represent *God* to *you!* The Word of God says that we, as believers, have been made kings and priests unto God (Rev. 1:6).

The Book of Hebrews reveals how Jesus became our High Priest.

If perfection could have been attained through the Levitical priesthood (for on the basis of it the law was given to the people), why was there still need for another priest to come — one in the order of Melchizedek, not in the order of Aaron? For when there is a change of the priesthood, there must also be a change of the law. He of whom these things are said belonged to a different tribe, and no one from that tribe has ever served at the altar. For it is clear that our Lord descended from Judah, and in regard to that tribe Moses said nothing about priests. And what we have said is even more clear if another priest like Melchizedek appears, one who has become a priest not on the basis of a regulation as to his ancestry but on the basis of the power of an indestructible life. For it is declared: "You are a priest forever, in the order of Melchizedek." The former regulation is set aside because it was weak and useless (for the law made nothing perfect), and a better hope is introduced, by which we draw near to God.

— Hebrews 7:11-19 (NIV)

You see, under the Old Covenant, the people could get to God only by going through the priest. But we don't have to go through anyone today. We don't have to go through a priest. We don't have to go through anyone except Jesus.

I came over among the Pentecostals in 1937. Then in 1940 there was a great controversy about firstfruits, tithes, and offerings. People believed that all the money belonged to the pastor. Well, some of us finally used some common sense and got straightened out. And God blessed us. But, you see, some people really had the idea that the pastor took in and handled all the money.

In fact, when I first started pastoring Pentecostal churches, I handled all of the church's money. But you can get into trouble doing that. You need some people to help you. This provides things honest in the sight of all men (Rom. 12:17). In one church I pastored, we had things set up very well. We had different funds for missions, building, buying flowers for the sick, and so on.

I remember one minister who became the pastor at a church I left. If I had known that church was going to consider him, I would have told them not to hire him. He didn't have a good record. He eventually stole every dime they had. They could have had him arrested for embezzlement. But as one of the deacons said, "We didn't want it in the paper." So they let him go, and eventually the church recovered.

Now some people are honest and sincere, but others are just trying to get more money. They don't have enough faith to believe God, so they try to work up some kind of system. They want all of the money to belong to them. Many people believe that all of the tithe belongs to the pastor. The last church I pastored thought that way. They said they wanted the Sunday morning and Sunday night offerings to go to me.

I said, "No, I'm doing real well; let's just take the Sunday night offering and put it in the church treasury because the church needs it."

The deacon board said, "We want you to have it."

"No," I said, "I don't need it. I'll take Sunday morning tithes and offerings, and we'll put the Sunday night offering into the general treasury because we need to do some building." This is probably a foreign concept to most people today. You see, in the 1940's churches were typically quite small. It was a common practice to give all the Sunday morning tithes and offerings to the pastor.

As a result of putting the Sunday night offering into the general treasury, we were able to remodel the front of the auditorium, add some Sunday school rooms, and fix up the youth hall.

All the money does not belong to the pastor. It's so easy to get in the ditch on one side or the other. Let's stay in the middle of the road.

Making a New Testament application of Old Testament technicalities violates every principle of Bible interpretation, especially when there isn't a single New Testament usage of the word "firstfruits" in the context in which it is being preached by some ministers.

The concept of firstfruits is not used in the New Testament in reference to financial giving. There is not even the vaguest hint of it by any New Testament writer in reference to money or the support of ministers.

"Firstfruits" in the New Testament primarily refers to Jesus Christ. He is the Firstfruits — the first One to be raised from the dead — and represented all those who would follow after him.

Other New Testament uses of "firstfruits" refer to the "firstfruits of the Spirit" in the life of the believer. In other words, "firstfruits" refers to the initial working of the Spirit in a believer's life — the first evidence of His indwelling us. It refers to those signs of His Presence in us now, as compared to what He will do with us later when we have our glorified bodies.

Another use of the word "firstfruits" is totally figurative. It has to do with the first individuals to be born again in a certain location.

After examining many teachings that have led to misunderstandings and hurtful problems in the Body of Christ, let's look at the Biblical way to prosper.

The Biblical Pattern — Receive and Give

One of the most interesting passages in the Old Testament describes how the Israelites who had been carried captive into Babylon finally were allowed to return home to Jerusalem. They gathered together inside the walls, Ezra the priest read to them from the Law of Moses, and the Levites explained it to them.

Let's read the account in Nehemiah chapter 8.

So they read in the book in the law of God distinctly, and gave the sense, and caused them to understand the reading . . . Then he said unto them, Go your way, eat the fat, and drink the sweet, and send portions unto them for whom nothing is prepared: for this day is holy unto our Lord: neither be ye sorry; for the joy of the Lord is your strength . . . And all the people went their way to eat, and to drink, and to send portions and to make great mirth, because they had understood the words that were declared unto them.

— Nehemiah 8:8,10,12

Notice what happened. After the people heard the Word of God, Nehemiah told them to celebrate with joy. They ate. They drank. They shared with those who had nothing.

In the New Testament, Jesus said to His disciples, "*. . . freely ye have received, freely give*" (Matt. 10:8). This is the biblical pattern. This is really what Christianity is all about. You receive, and then you give.

Let's look at another scripture passage that mentions giving to the poor.

Is not this the fast that I have chosen? to loose the bands of wickedness, to undo the heavy burdens, and to let the oppressed go free, and that ye break every yoke? Is it not to deal thy bread to the hungry, and that thou bring the poor that are cast out to thy house? when thou seest the naked, that thou cover him; and that thou hide not thyself from thine own flesh? Then shall thy light break forth as the morning, and thine health shall spring forth speedily: and thy righteousness shall go before thee; the glory of the Lord shall be thy rereward.

— Isaiah 58:6-8

What impression do you get from these verses about the reward of giving to the poor? Will the giver just get back what he gives or a bountiful reward?

As I mentioned earlier, one of the ideas put forth by some preachers is that because they are Jesus' representatives and anointed like Him, you are to give to them *personally* in order to get a greater return on your giving. Is this *in agreement with* or *contrary to* what Jesus and Paul taught under the inspiration of the Holy Spirit in the New Testament?

What Jesus Said About Giving to the Poor

Some of the money-oriented doctrine going around implies that only highly anointed ministers represent the Lord.

Let's read in the Gospel of Matthew to find out who represents the Lord.

Then shall the King say unto them on his right hand,
Come, ye blessed of my Father, inherit the kingdom pre-
pared for you from the foundation of the world: For I
was an hungered, and ye gave me meat: I was thirsty,
and ye gave me drink: I was a stranger, and ye took me
in:Naked, and ye clothed me: I was sick, and ye visited
me: I was in prison, and ye came unto me. Then shall
the righteous answer him, saying, Lord, when saw we
thee an hungered, and fed thee? or thirsty, and gave thee
drink? When saw we thee a stranger, and took thee in?
or naked, and clothed thee? Or when saw we thee sick,
or in prison, and came unto thee? And the King shall
answer and say unto them, Verily I say unto you,
Inasmuch as ye have done it unto one of the least of these
my brethren, ye have done it unto me.

— Matthew 25:34-40

Notice here that Jesus said *He was represented by the poor!*

When Jesus appeared to Saul of Tarsus, who was perse-
cuting the Church at large, He said to him, "*Saul, Saul, why*
persecutest thou me?" (Acts 9:4). In this instance, Jesus said *He*
was represented by the whole Church.

Jesus Himself, in unmistakable terms, declared that poor
Christians and the whole Body of Christ at large represent
Him just as much as a fivefold minister!

In First Corinthians 10:31, the Apostle Paul wrote, *"Whether therefore ye eat, or drink, or whatsoever ye do, do all to the glory of God."* So when you give to the poor, do it as unto the Lord. God will bless that. When you tithe and give offerings to your church, do it as unto the Lord. God will bless that. When you give an offering personally to a minister or to anyone else, do it as unto the Lord. God will bless that.

Realize that you don't have to respond to some sensationalized, goose-bump-raising offering in order to give productively and effectively into the Body of Christ! Paul instructed us to give as we purpose in our heart. Sure, there may be occasions when we are led by the Spirit of God to support a particular individual or cause. We should obey the Spirit of God.

But most of the time, we should be systematic in our giving. We should support our local churches on purpose with our tithes. We should find ministries that are producing good results and purpose to sow faithfully into those ministries.

Any giving may be *profitable* to the giver, and any giving may be *unprofitable* to the giver. What counts is that the giver *does it as unto the Lord.*

Will There Be an End-Time Transfer of Wealth?

There has been quite a bit of discussion in the last couple of years about a coming transference of wealth from the world to the Church. The idea is based on part of a scripture that says, ". . . *the wealth of the sinner is laid up for the just*" (Prov. 13:22). Apparently, some have interpreted this to mean that the day will come when God's people will have plenty of money for the work of God — money transferred to us from the wealth of the worldly.

First of all, I really don't see anything about this in the New Testament, especially in terms of what we are supposed to be actively believing God for. And I'm always wary about building a doctrine or basic belief on a single scripture. Jesus said, ". . . *in the mouth of two or three witnesses every word may be established*" (Matt. 18:16).

I'm sure that as the Church does its job and gets people born again, there will be more people giving their tithes and offerings for the work of the Lord. But I think we need to be careful about coveting the world's money. We shouldn't be so concerned about getting sinners' money transferred into our hands. Our concern should be getting their hearts transferred into the Kingdom. We should be focused on their receiving what we have (eternal life), not on our receiving what they have (material goods).

Paul said to the Corinthians, "I seek not *yours*, but *you*" (2 Cor. 12:14). As a minister, he was not focused on their money, but on their souls.

The Apostle John said the following about some ministers who traveled with the Gospel: *"Because that for his name's sake they went forth, taking nothing of the Gentiles"* (3 John 7).

Other translations of this verse emphasize the point:

". . . accepting nothing from the heathen" (*Goodspeed*)

". . . taking nothing from the people of the world" (*Beck*)

". . . and declined to take anything from pagans" (*Moffatt*)

". . . and they accept no help from non-Christians" (*Phillips*)

Our job is not to try to get the wealth of the world. Our job is to faithfully use the wealth we already have to get the Gospel out. If all Christians would simply tithe and give offerings, the Church would have more than enough funds to accomplish whatever it needs to do. Statistics indicate that twenty percent of church members provide eighty percent of church revenue and that the average American Christian gives only six percent of his income to the Lord's work. Imagine where we would be if those percentages were where they ought to be!

The Bible does teach that when the Church returns with Jesus after the Tribulation and He sets up His Millennial Kingdom on earth, we will be inheriting all of the wealth of the sinners at that time. I don't see anywhere in the New Testament where we are supposed to be *focused* on getting their money now. Instead, we should be concentrating on seeking the hearts of the unsaved and faithfully using the finances we already have.

The Use of Gimmicks

Looking back over more than sixty-five years of ministry, I can remember a lot of gimmicks preachers have used to attract attention and get a larger response from people to their ads and appeals. Although you might suppose there are a lot of new gimmicks today, a great many of them have been around for decades. I've seen some of them come and go two or three times.

Some gimmicks are absolutely ridiculous, and the fact that they seem to work just illustrates how unlearned and superstitious many people are. They are prisoners of the soul-ish realm and do not live in the spiritual realm.

Years ago, someone on the radio talked about a red string he would send you for an offering of $10. It was supposed to have special power in it. If you were fat, wearing the string around your waist would cause you to lose weight. If you were skinny, wearing the red string would help you gain weight.

Then someone came up with the idea of blessed billfolds that had been prayed over. People could get them by sending the minister a $25 offering. People were supposed to put the billfold in their pocket and expect God to miraculously fill it up with money. After carrying it a while, people were supposed to open the blessed billfold and find that money had been sup-plied to pay their bills.

I know it seems impossible that anyone would be deceived by something so silly, but many sent in their money and used those red strings and blessed billfolds. Other gimmicks may seem more believable and convincing.

Back in the 1950s, I heard a radio preacher ask people to send him an offering and a prayer request. He promised to take every letter of request that he received with him on a trip to Jerusalem and pray over them in the empty tomb where Jesus had been buried. I heard that he got sackfuls of mail; thousands of people wanted him to pray over their requests in that special place.

There is absolutely nothing in the Scriptures to suggest that God will hear and answer a prayer from the tomb in Jerusalem anymore than He will hear you praying in your bedroom, or at work, or anywhere else where you cry out to Him in faith. The important thing is not who prays where, but that you believe God, based on His Word.

The Jerusalem prayer deal was simply another gimmick. What that radio preacher really wanted was more people to send in offerings. And he wanted more names he could put on his mailing list to promote with other mailings and appeals.

Sometimes the gimmick is very subtle, and even the person promoting it may be deceived into thinking that what he's doing is genuine. A few months ago, I was glancing through a church paper that had been sent to me (I get a lot of them).

One of the upcoming meetings the church was promoting was a special "double portion" night. It said, "Come believing and receive your double portion!"

This item got my attention because I remembered hearing about "double portion" services fifty years ago. It seemed like one person thought of doing it, and then everyone across the country got on the bandwagon.

The problem with "double portion" services is that the idea that every believer can receive a double portion from the Lord is not scriptural. A double portion of what?

The concept is developed from the Old Testament story about Elisha and Elijah, who were both called and anointed in the office of prophet. Elijah said, "Ask what I shall do for you before I be taken away from you" (2 Kings 2:9). Elisha answered by saying he wanted a double portion of Elijah's spirit.

The rest of the account tells how Elisha met the condition of seeing Elijah go up in the chariot of fire and how the mantle of Elijah fell on him. And the biblical record shows that Elisha *did* receive a double portion of Elijah's anointing, and he performed twice as many miracles.

There are at least two reasons, or conditions, that qualified Elisha to receive a double portion. First, he was called and anointed to be a prophet, just like Elijah was. And second, Elijah told him to ask for what he wanted from him.

What qualifies the people at one of today's special "double portion" services to be asking for a double portion? Are they asking for a double portion of material things? Or are they asking for a double portion of spiritual things? Either way, there's no biblical basis for it at all. God has already promised to provide all their needs. How can they get a double portion of *all?*

Every believer has an anointing of the Spirit within. The Bible says, *"But the anointing which ye have received of him abideth in you . . ."* (1 John 2:27).

So why have a "double portion" service? No doubt most ministers who use this idea want it to be a blessing to people, but they may well be promising something they can't deliver. And part of the reason for scheduling the special service is to get more people to attend and participate in the church service.

I believe ministers need to be really careful about what they sponsor and promote. And they always need to be sure their motives are pure.

[1]Gordon Lindsay, *The Charismatic Ministry,* Christ for the Nations, Inc., Dallas, 1983, pp. 51-52. Used by permission.

[2]Ibid., pp. 50-51.

[3]Gordon Lindsay, "Ten Rules We Must Follow If We Are to See a World-Shaking Revival," *The Voice of Healing,* November 1949, p. 12. Used by permission.

[4]Donald Gee, *Wind and Flame* (rev. and enlarged ed. [Springfield, Mo.]: Assemblies of God Publishing House, 1967).

[5]Donald Gee, *A Way To Escape,* Gospel Publishing House, Springfield, Mo., 1966, p. 31. Used by permission.

177

C H A P T E R   S E V E N

BALANCE AND SOUND TEACHING

Throughout this book, I have tried to stress the importance of providing a proper emphasis on important Christian truths. On so many of these issues, there have been people who emphasized a particular idea or concept so much that they carried it to an extreme. Their attitude seemed to be, if a little bit of this is *good*, then a whole lot must be *better*.

When this happened, usually another group rose up to correct the overemphasis. Unfortunately, often their "correction" was to the opposite extreme — because "too much" of this idea is so offensive, let's get rid of it altogether. You might say they tended to "throw the baby out with the bath water."

The result was that a great gulf was created between the two extreme positions, and often misunderstandings and animosity arose. People in both camps got so caught up in the conflict that they forgot the original motivation of both sides, which was to do good and bless people. And in their overzealousness, both sides often lost sight of the original truth!

My way of describing this is to call the basic truth — the biblical position — the middle of the road, and the extreme applications as the ditches on either side of the road. It has been my experience that a person doesn't have to travel very far before he sees people off in a ditch on one side of the road or the other. For some reason, it seems like the hardest thing in the world for the Body of Christ to stay balanced on a subject.

Take note that it is not just bad people who get into a ditch. Good people — sincere, well-meaning Christian believers whose zealousness for the truth is commendable can allow their zeal to exceed their wisdom. I believe that even some of the Christian leaders whose failures made national headlines in past years did not intentionally set out to hurt anyone or to fall into error. They went out on tangents and got away from the main purpose and central truth of the Gospel. Once off track, it was all too easy to go downhill in a hurry.

Let's look at some examples of basic Bible truths and their extreme applications — the middle of the road position and the ditches on either side of the road.

Subject	Error and Extreme *The Ditch on One Side of the Road*	The Truth *The Middle Of the Road*	Error and Extreme *Ditch on the Other Side of the Road*
Water Baptism	You can't be saved unless you're baptized using a special formula.	Baptism is an ordinance of the Church that communicates our identification with Christ's death, burial, and resurrection.	Baptism has no relevance or importance today whatsoever.
Divine Healing	Healing has been done away with. The day of miracles is past.	God does heal today, but natural means of help are appropriate and acceptable also.	Divine healing is the only legitimate way to go. Using doctors or medicine is a sin.
Ministry Gifts	We don't need pastors and ministers any longer. God is going to use everyone equally.	The ministry gifts Christ gave are still here today. Their job is to equip the saints to do the work of the ministry and to further each Christian's walk with God by feeding them the Word.	Those with ministry gifts are a superior class of Christians. They should rule over all other Christians and run not only the church, but also the lives of all believers.

Do you recognize some or all of the varying positions on these basic issues? You may be aware of some extreme views on other doctrinal points as well. Finding, and staying, in a balanced position on basic issues such as these is obviously not an easy task. To this day, some churches struggle to stay out of the ditches of error when it comes to administering the ministry gifts.

Ministry Gifts Should Produce Balance

One of the pioneers of Pentecostalism who helped the movement get established on a firm biblical foundation was an Englishman named Donald Gee. He spoke so eloquently about the problems of extremism and excesses that he became known as the "Apostle of Balance." I was privileged to meet him many years ago and hear him speak. I read many of his articles and books and always found them to be full of wisdom and insight. I loved and appreciated his ministry.

In the 1930s Gee wrote the following profound counsel about how the ministry gifts interact to produce balance and soundness.

One of the most charming things that meet us on the very threshold of studies on the ministry-gifts of Christ, is their wise variety.

It is true that the first on the list, the apostle, seems to embrace almost every type of ministry; but there are prophets, whose ministry is inspirational and appeals to the emotional elements of human nature; and then to balance these are teachers, whose ministry is logical and appeals to the intellectual faculties. . . . Then there are evangelists whose ministry will be almost exclusively *without* [outside] the church: and pastors whose ministry will be almost exclusively *within* the church — both equally needed and honorable.

This matter of balance in ministry is vitally important to effective, aggressive ministry without, and well-rounded growth within; far more important than most believers realize. Many assemblies have no vision but that of a one-man ministry, which is expected to fulfill every requirement — evangelistic, pastoral, teaching, prophetic. One man is expected to have marked success in evangelism, be a splendid organizer, a good pastoral visitor, a competent Bible teacher, possessing in addition gifts of healing and inspired utterance. The marvel is that so many men seem to approximate at least in some measure to these exorbitant and un-Scriptural demands. Usually it is at terrific strain to themselves; and it may easily result in their never reaching a first-class competence in what *is* their truly God-given line of ministry.

Other assemblies and individuals do not even seem to have the desire or vision for one man to fill every needed line of ministry; they only appear to see one line of ministry, and have neither time, nor appreciation, nor encouragement for anything beyond their own line of things. For instance, some assemblies and individual believers have no vision or enthusiasm for anything but evangelism in the narrowest sense of that term, and almost ignore teaching and teachers. On the opposite hand, there are others who would, if they had their way, have so much Bible teaching that they would turn any assembly into little more than a Bible school, and completely ignore an aggressive outside testimony. Both the above types may quite likely unite in "despising prophesyings" (1 Thessalonians 5:20), and have no time nor place for the gifts of prophecy, tongues, or interpretation. Yet at the other extreme there are those who place such an undue value and importance upon these very gifts that they do not consider a preacher to be in the blessing and liberty of the Spirit at all unless his ministry is continually sprinkled with manifestations of this description; and they like every meeting of the assembly to be dominated by these features. In each and every case there is a serious lack of balance.

What is needed is an appreciation of the *varied* ministries Christ has placed in the church, and a realization that each and all of them are essential to well-rounded activity and growth. It is no uncommon thing to hear teachers disparage evangelists by calling them "superficial" or "sensational": and then to hear evangelists stigmatize teachers as being "stodgy" and "dry." Both types may unite in calling prophets fanatical and extreme; and then the inspirational folk retaliate by calling the equally God-given ministry of their brethren "carnal" and "fleshly" when, rightly understood, it is nothing of the kind. All such attitudes are wrong.

It is perfectly true that there can be extremes in evangelism which *are* superficial: there can be extremes in teaching which *are* heavy and barren: there can be extremes in prophesying which *are* most undeniably fanatical. Yet the true remedy is not to be found in repressing therefore any particular one of these lines of diverse ministry, for thereby we may all too easily quench the Spirit of God also. Indeed this has been actually done too often; men have dealt with the false and unprofitable at the terrible expense of cutting out the real at the same time. It needs an inspired touch to regulate inspired ministry. *The divine plan is for each and every ministry which God has set in the church to correct and complement the other, thereby providing just the elements lacking and just the check needed to restore overbalanced tendencies on any one line — the prophet to inspire the teacher, the teacher to steady the prophet; the evangelist to continually remind us of the needy world outside dying for the gospel, the pastor to show us that souls still need much caring for even after they have been "won." The apostle above all to inspire and lead the way to fresh conquests for Christ and His church.* [The emphasis in the previous two sentences is mine.][1]

Some seventy years later, this is still a wonderful word for the Church. Indeed, "the matter of balance in ministry is vitally important — far more important than most believers realize."

The Money Balance

Now let's talk about the issue of balance when it comes to money. Again, people tend to end up in one of three positions:

Error and Extreme *The Ditch on One* *Side of the Road*	The Truth *The Middle* *Of the Road*	Error and Extreme *Ditch on the Other* *Side of the Road*
• Money is an evil that all Christians should avoid. • God wants His children to be poor. • Poverty shows humility. • Preachers should never talk about money.	• God wants to bless and prosper His children. • We are to seek first the Kingdom of God as opposed to being materialistically oriented. • Preachers should teach the truth of God's Word about money, but they shouldn't be self-serving. • Preachers should keep their teaching on prosperity in balance with the many other truths of God's Word.	• Getting rich is the main focus of faith. • God's main interest is your material well-being. • Material gain shows godliness. • Preachers should teach about money more than any other subject.

I often have the opportunity to talk with pastors from all over the country. They tell me that one of the greatest frustrations they face is determining how to maintain balance on the issue of prosperity and financial blessings. If they stress keeping motives pure and not becoming covetous or greedy, it seems that people have trouble believing God for material things. On the other hand, if they stress and emphasize believing God for prosperity, people often tend to get overly materialistic.

Again, those who get off into a ditch on this issue are not necessarily bad people. But even sincere, honest people can allow their zeal for truth to exceed their wisdom.

Pursuing Truth in a Balanced Way

A friend of mine, Bob Buess, published a book in 1975 entitled, *The Pendulum Swings*. A Baptist minister who received the infilling of the Holy Spirit, Brother Buess was also out on the evangelistic field during the same years I was, and from time to time, we would run into each other and have good fellowship together. His book has some important things to say about pursuing spiritual truth in a balanced, loving way, avoiding a legalistic, dogmatic spirit. In the preface to his book, Buess writes the following (all emphases are mine):

A few years ago I was interested in a certain teaching, so I began to pursue the Word of God to find more on this subject. I believed the Bible from cover to cover, but I allowed myself to disregard certain Scriptures. I blanked out certain truths. My mind became completely indifferent to certain verses in the Word.

My new dogma was no different from the old, but I began to defend my new doctrine. It was, in a subtle way, becoming a god which I had to defend and protect.

I was not an unusual case. It's easy for Christians to pursue a thought which the Holy Spirit aroused in them as they studied the Scriptures. In their excitement, they set out to explore the Word of God to see what could be found. When they find a few Scriptures to support this new-found idea, they soon can be running madly through the Bible trying to prove their theory.

Dogmatism begins to set in. Without fully realizing what they are doing, these people jump verses, throw out some, and ignore others to prove their point. . . .

People driven by this cause rush madly on in a pursuit of new arguments to promote their theory. As time passes they become harsh. . . .

The purpose of this book is to cause the reader to *slow down and look at the other side of some issues* facing Christians today. It is to let the pendulum swing back into the will of God rather than let it be hung up in dogmas and legalism. It is to call for a re-examination of present studies from a non-partisan viewpoint. It is a call to take seriously James 3:1 which condemns the teacher who dogmatically rushes ahead without balance in his teaching.

The Apostle Paul wrote a letter to the Galatian Christians who were leaving the simplicity of the gospel and reverting to rules and regulations. That Galatian spirit is working in the Body of Christ today, causing some believers to be legalistic in their approach to the Word and to be hard and dogmatic in dealing with truth and with people. . . .

People are caught up in confusion and error simply because *teachers have rushed headlong into pet doctrines with no regard for the other side.*

Seeing the other side requires that we pursue wisdom. Proverbs 4:7 says: *"Wisdom is the principal thing, therefore get wisdom, and with all thy getting get understanding.* . . . Jesus Christ Himself will deliver us from legalism, for He is wisdom (1 Corinthians 1:30).[2]

I believe Buess's insightful comments still apply to us today and we would be wise to consider them.

Extremes Are Sometimes Necessary

One problem I've seen through the years concerning the Church is that people holding different beliefs on spiritual issues often begin warring over their positions. I saw this happen first-hand during the days of the Healing Revival, which was from 1947 to 1958. Before it was over, extremism and error actually destroyed the ministry (and life) of more than one talented and effective man. And the momentum of that great revival was stopped when great numbers of people were disappointed and hurt by the excesses of some of its leaders.

Early in the revival, Donald Gee wrote an article in *The Voice of Healing* issuing a call for reason and responsibility. The article was entitled, "Extremes Are Sometimes Necessary." I have included it in its entirety (all emphases are mine).

One of the paradoxes of the truly Pentecostal witness is its emphasis upon the necessity of maintaining a proper balance in doctrine and practice, coupled with a complementary testimony that often urges to extremes in both.

Paul's teaching concerning spiritual gifts is all for balance and moderation — "I will sing with the spirit and I will sing with the understanding also"; We are to avoid giving any impression of being "mad"; "By two, or at the most by three"; "God is not the author of confusion, but of peace"; "Let all things be done decently and in order" (1 Cor. 14:15, 23,27,33,40). Yet at the same time he affirms in extreme language that he speaks with tongues more than they all; expresses a vehement preference for teaching at a ratio of 10,000 to 5; and says "ye may all prophesy" (1 Cor. 14:18,19,31). . . .

So many of us are inveterate [firmly established] extremists. If we see any ray of truth we push it to such an extreme that our constant pressing of it becomes offensive, vain and at last erroneous. If we discover any successful line of ministry we run after it to such an extent that it becomes nauseating and exhausted. We are for ever missing genuine usefulness by our constant failure to keep well-balanced. In the end men lose confidence in us, our intemperance grieves the Holy Spirit, and we are cast upon the scrap-heap of rejected and unprofitable servants.

But still more of us are in danger of missing a life of power by seeking to walk in monotonous middle-course that never ventures to an extreme at all. Our preaching lacks fire because it always is trying to present both sides of a case at the same time, and our methods are ineffective because they eschew [avoid] any offense against respectability or tradition. We may, if we like, pride our-selves upon our success in avoiding disaster but our safety has been achieved by remaining static. We have made practically no impact upon the community. If it be true that they have never charged us with madness it also is true that they never have reported that God is among us of a truth. Most probably they do not even know of our existence!

We rightly extol the importance of balance; we correctly affirm that the way of truth will not be found in extremes; we justly point out that persistent extremism is suicidal for both men and movements — but we desperate-ly need to recognize that revivals are never launched with-out someone going to an extreme. Passionate intercession is positively unbalanced; so is much fasting; so is fervent preaching that makes sinners tremble; and feverish itinerating that makes a missionary or an evangelist seem beside himself. We do well to remember that our Lord's Own kinsmen thought that He had gone mad (Mark 3:21); and that He quoted "The zeal of Thine house hath eaten me up" (John 2:17) when He kicked over the table of the money-changers.

The Day of Pentecost so disturbed the emotional balance of the disciples that they seemed like drunken men. . . . Thirty years later a Roman Governor accused Paul of being mad. The charge was courteously and properly refuted but let us admit that Festus was no fool. Paul himself testified that at times he was beside himself (2 Cor. 5:13), and his superb sanity of teaching and outlook operated on a heavenly level.

There HAS to be an extremism to move things. . . . Miracles of healing occur when faith refuses to be logical, and blinds itself to arguments, based on plenty of contrary experience and more "balanced" teaching. Indeed we may well enquire whether there is not something extreme in any genuine miracle.

Where, then, lies the way of Pentecostal truth that embraces *a legitimate extremism* and *an essential balance?* I can only reply that *we need the extremist to start things moving, but we need the balanced teacher to keep them moving in the right direction. We need extremism for a miracle of healing, but we need balanced sanity for health. We need extreme fervor to launch a movement, but we need the repudiation of extremes to save it from self-destruction. Only a wisdom from above can reveal the perfect synthesis. It takes Pentecostal genius to know when and where an extreme doctrine or practice must be modified to a more balanced view; and where, on the other hand, the broad lines of truth must be temporarily narrowed into an extreme emphasis upon one point to ensure a dynamic powerful enough to move things for God.* The possession of that uncommon genius marks the God-sent leader who has emerged in truly great periods of revival.[3]

Extreme Emphases

In the past we have seen extreme emphases in many different areas of doctrine. Let's look at a few of these and then examine both the positive purposes and the dangers regarding extreme emphases.

We have seen an extreme emphasis in the faith movement. Some people have thought all believers should throw away their medicine and refuse to go to a doctor, cancel all their insurance policies, quit their jobs to "live by faith," and never borrow money under any circumstances.

We have seen an extreme emphasis on the move of the Holy Ghost. Some people have thought they were never supposed to have any kind of service other than a Holy Ghost meeting with people laughing and rolling on the floor *every time* they came to church.

Others have thought *every minister* was supposed to be holding Holy Ghost meetings all the time.

We have seen an extreme emphasis on teaching that prosperity — especially material prosperity — is for Christians. Some have come to believe that demonstrating prosperity involves displaying a lavish, ostentatious lifestyle rather than being good stewards and efficiently harnessing abundant resources to promote the Gospel and to minister the goodness of God to all who are in need.

However, an extreme emphasis alone is not what causes problems. Sometimes an extreme emphasis is necessary to shock and awaken a sleeping, lethargic, and apathetic church to recognize a neglected truth that is necessary for progress to be made.

Often an extreme emphasis involves people in one ditch trying to pull another group of people out of the ditch on the other side of the road.

An extreme emphasis then, simply excites people and stirs them up about a general truth that has been neglected or ignored. An extreme emphasis should get our attention. But then we need wisdom to make a productive and fruitful *application* of that general truth.

The problem is created when there is an extreme application made of what has been emphasized. In other words, people have failed to make a balanced application of what has been heavily emphasized. They have failed to integrate that truth into the rest of God's Word. The whole counsel of God's Word is what will keep us in balance.

So how does a minister integrate a certain truth that the Holy Spirit is emphasizing into the whole of the Word of God? I believe the answer is, *by consciously presenting a balanced view of the subject, searching out as many scriptural foundation stones as possible, not just teaching on an isolated verse.*

Even if ministers or students of the Word focus on a particular truth, it is still important to include other subjects in their spiritual diet. Just because a child prefers dessert, the wise parent does not fail to also put bread, meat, and vegetables on his plate.

I have followed a rule of thumb that has served me well in presenting the whole counsel of God's Word. If the Bible gives a subject a lot of emphasis, with many verses in different books of the Bible, I've tried to emphasize that subject in my preaching and teaching. If the Bible says very little about another subject, I've made it a point not to place an extreme amount of emphasis on that subject or to be overly dogmatic concerning it.

Don't Abandon Practical Wisdom and Common Sense

Not only should we as Christians apply biblical teaching and spiritual principles in our day-to-day living, but we also must not abandon practical wisdom and common sense. There must be balance in this part of our lives as well.

The faith walk does not ignore the natural laws of the universe, which actually are God's laws. As a rule, God does not supernaturally perform what we have the power to do for ourselves. Most people discover that only after they have done all they know and have the power to do does God step in and do what only He can do.

For example, there is no question that God can miraculously heal our human bodies. I personally was raised up from my deathbed and made completely whole. Over the years, I have seen many people healed of everything from headaches to cancers.

Just because God can and does heal doesn't mean that we shouldn't use common sense in taking care of our bodies, eating the right foods, exercising, working in a reasonable way, and getting proper rest. Nor should a person with a disease stop his medical treatment and abandon all reason and common sense. It would be folly, not faith, for a person with diabetes to keep eating large quantities of starchy, sugary foods, saying that he was trusting God to heal him.

In the same sense, it would be ridiculous for people to try to "look prosperous" by buying all kinds of luxurious items and charging them to credit cards that already have payments they can't afford. "I believe God is going to provide the money to pay off my debts somehow, some way," they say. "I'm expecting a miracle blessing. Maybe He'll help me to win the lottery!"

Obviously these people's expectations are based on mistaken understandings and wrong motives. There is no balance between faith and reality in their lives. With so little wisdom and spiritual discernment to draw upon, these people are easily deceived and led further astray by misguided or unscrupulous religious promoters.

Is Prosperity Tied Solely to Giving?

In teaching prosperity, too many preachers seem to communicate the idea that receiving financial abundance is totally and exclusively tied to one thing — giving…usually to *them*! Don't misunderstand me. I believe in giving. I believe that giving is important. But it is not the only key to prosperity.

My son, Rev. Kenneth Hagin Jr., is pastor of RHEMA Bible Church in Broken Arrow, Oklahoma. From time to time, he preaches about prosperity to his congregation, which includes a large number of young people, many of them students at RHEMA Bible Training Center. Ken includes a lot of scriptures from the Word of God that define prosperity and show that it is definitely included in God's will for His people today. As part of the Bible lesson, Ken teaches about tithing and giving as vital elements of biblical prosperity.

He also stresses that knowing and doing what the Bible says has a direct relationship to our prosperity. Joshua 1:8 declares, "*This book of the law* [the Word of God] *shall not depart out of thy mouth; but thou shalt meditate therein day and night, that thou mayest observe to do according to all that is written therein: for then thou shalt make thy way prosperous, and then thou shalt have good success.*"

You see, the Bible doesn't just speak about God prospering us. The Bible also speaks of us making our own way prosperous. That's why Ken doesn't deal with just the spiritual aspect of prosperity. He also encourages young people to identify their skills and interests and to then seek God as to how He might be leading them vocationally. They should get the best education they possibly can and gain a broad range of knowledge about the world they live in. He advises adults who would like to advance on their jobs to take classes and get extra training.

Ken also teaches people to work hard and to be diligent in performing their duties on their jobs. In most cases, workers who take an interest in their work and do a good job are recognized and rewarded for what they do. It's true that we should trust in God as our Source rather than placing all our confidence in a job or the economy. But that doesn't mean that financial prosperity is totally unrelated to a person's occupation.

While God can channel blessings to us from many sources, much of the time He uses our job as the primary channel. Typically, there is a direct relationship between one's personal financial prosperity and the amount of responsibility he or she takes on at work. Folks who work harder and in more specialized, skilled fields — those whose abilities are in greater demand — receive a greater financial reward.

Paul told the Thessalonians, ". . . *work with your own hands, as we commanded you; That ye may walk honestly toward them that are without, and that ye may have lack of nothing* (1 Thess. 4:11,12).

He also declared, "*And whatsoever ye do, do it heartily, as to the Lord, and not unto men*" (Col. 3:23).

Another important lesson Ken teaches his congregation is the importance of good associations. You can't stay around people who are filled with doubt and unbelief without doubt and unbelief rubbing off on you. You can't be with people who are critical and complaining all the time without being affected. You can't associate with people who lie and cheat without being tempted to compromise your own moral character. Back in the days when people burned wood or coal in stoves, there was an old saying, "You can't handle a stove pipe without getting your hands dirty."

The Whole Counsel of God's Word

I believe pastors and teachers have a responsibility to teach the full Word of God, not just one part. All of the things Ken includes as part of his teaching on prosperity help bring a balance to the subject that isn't obtained by just talking about giving.

Some people become religiously imbalanced, stressing and practicing only certain truths and neglecting or ignoring others. Sooner than later, we need to learn that the Bible doesn't teach a lopsided, imbalanced message regarding prosperity. There is much more to the message than constantly saying, "If you want to be prosperous, give! If you want to be prosperous, give! If you want to be prosperous, give!"

Ministers who do this are not teaching the whole counsel of God. In my personal opinion, they do an injustice to the Word of God by emphasizing just one side of the issue. They give understandable grounds to those who charge that their motive is to get people to give to them. Is it possible that their full confidence is not in the promises of the Word and they feel they have to "help" God, constantly trying to raise money by asking for it from others?

Another crucially important issue is that ministers should never suggest or lead people to believe that prosperity means conspicuous, lavish wealth. It simply is not true that everyone who has faith for prosperity will live in a palace, drive a luxurious car, and dress in expensive, designer-label clothes.

Prosperity is relative. For some people, being able to pay their bills and provide the basic comforts of life for their families would be a great blessing — a definite step up. In some countries, being prosperous might mean having a bicycle or motorcycle to ride, or an ox to plow the fields to plant a crop.

Why Does God Prosper Us?

God sends prosperity to bless us and meet our needs. But even more important, He prospers us to make it possible for us to help carry out His work in our communities, our nation, and throughout the earth. If we fail to understand this, or forget it, I believe we run the risk of losing the blessing.

Over the years, RHEMA Bible Training Center has sent out thousands of workers into the harvest. Many graduates are pastoring or working in helps ministries in local churches. Many others are on the mission field carrying out the call of God on their lives. One of the great joys of my life is getting reports from our former students about what they are doing in the work of the Lord.

In this way, we have heard many testimonies from people in various developing nations who have heard the Gospel and have given their hearts to God. As they began to believe and practice God's Word, they also began to experience prosperity, or increase, in their lives. The things they were thankful for might not seem like very much to people in developed nations, but just having clean water for their children or a roof that didn't leak represented a dramatic improvement for them.

I remember one national missions leader testifying that when he began working in one area, none of the national pastors or evangelists under his supervision had any transportation except walking. As he began teaching them about the principles of prosperity and believing God to supply their needs, in just a year or so, every national minister in his district had either a bicycle or motorcycle, or some other motorized vehicle. This made it so much easier and more convenient for them to get to different villages to preach Jesus and share the Good News of the Gospel. Now these people still were not wealthy by the standards of some, but they considered themselves blessed and prosperous!

Prosperity is not an "American gospel." It will work in Africa, India, China, or anywhere else God's people practice the truth of His Word. If it's not true in the poorest place on earth, it's not true at all!

Why have people in America and other developed nations been blessed with more material resources than other countries? I don't know the complete answer. I do know that we have so much to be thankful for. Anyone who has traveled to the underdeveloped nations can confirm that even our poorest citizens have more than most of the world's people.

Perhaps one reason we have been entrusted with so many resources is so we can finance the worldwide fulfillment of Christ's Great Commission and do other good works. Surely we do have a responsibility to share our blessings. Jesus said, ". . . *For unto whomsoever much is given, of him shall be much required: and to whom men have committed much, of him they will ask the more* (Luke 12:48).

The Apostle James declared, "*Therefore to him that knoweth to do good, and doeth it not, to him it is sin*" (James 4:17). May God help us not to fail to do the good that is in our power to do.

Be Good Stewards By Being Informed

Not only do we have an obligation to bless others and help finance taking the Gospel into all the world, but we are also responsible to invest our funds into ministries that are trustworthy and productive. Like a farmer, we should do our best to determine that we are sowing our seeds into good ground.

As I have said, I believe a Christian's first consideration and priority in giving should be to his local church. The tithe should go to the church to support the ministers and the outreaches of that assembly of believers.

Second, believers can and should also support other ministries from which they receive spiritual food and that they have committed to "partner with." This support should come from offerings over and above the tithe.

I believe our basic giving should be planned and systematic. Paul urged believers to give as they "purposed in their hearts." That means they should be giving on purpose, rather than from an emotional appeal, from guilt, or on some impulse. Giving "as the Spirit leads" is fine, but that should be done in addition to one's planned and systematic giving, not in place of it. A church needs consistent and regular support it can count on in order to keep its work and programs running smoothly. Erratic and inconsistent giving by members makes it difficult for the church to plan and maintain a budget.

Ministries that function outside, but in support of, the local church also depend on consistent and systematic gifts. One-time or occasional gifts are welcome and appreciated, but an organization like Kenneth Hagin Ministries also needs a regular revenue flow it can count on. This is the purpose of our Word Partner Club, where friends commit to send regular gifts on a monthly basis.

Believers should look for organizations to support that are productive for the Kingdom of God, ministries that are actively contributing to the preaching of the Gospel and the expansion of the Church. A prospective giver might ask questions such as the following:

How many people are being born again and filled with the Spirit through this ministry?

How many people are being established and strengthened in the faith through its outreaches?

Is multiplication taking place? Are ministers being produced and churches being established?

Is good being accomplished in the world and in the Body of Christ through this ministry?

Is its message one of truth?

Is the ministry a good steward of its finances?

Are the methods used in ministry and in fundraising ethical and wholesome?

Is the ministry (and its ministers) financially accountable?

There are also some "red flags" or warning signs to watch for in determining whether a ministry is sound and worthy of support. I would suggest the utmost caution in supporting or being involved with any organization that has the following marks:

Exerts pressure to give or encourages impulse giving by saying, "You must give now!"

Makes suggestions of condemnation and guilt if you don't give.

Uses hype, emotionalism, and spiritual manipulation, such as "prophesying" dollars out of your pocket.

Makes outlandish promises such as, "Everyone who gives now will receive a hundredfold return." Or, "Those who give to this offering will have your debts cancelled."

Does not promote the local church, or projects the idea that theirs is the only ministry worth supporting.

Spends more time and energy raising funds than in doing the work of the ministry.

Builds money appeals around gimmicks and sensationalism.

Let's strive to maintain balance in every area, including the area of finances and prosperity. Remember to look to the whole counsel of God's Word while not neglecting practical wisdom and common sense. This will help you stay in the middle of the road at all times.

---

[1]Donald Gee, *The Ministry-Gifts of Christ,* Gospel Publishing House, Springfield, Mo., 1930, pp. 21-25. Used by permission.

[2]Bob Buess, *The Pendulum Swings,* New Leaf Press, Harrison, Ark., 1975, pp. 9-10. Used by permission.

[3]Donald Gee, "Extremes Are Sometimes Necessary," *The Voice of Healing,* April 1953, p. 9. Used by permission.

CHAPTER EIGHT

TWENTY-FOUR PRINCIPLES FROM THE EPISTLES REGARDING MONEY, GIVING, AND RECEIVING

I am a great advocate of the New Testament, especially the Epistles. Throughout my years in the ministry, I've tried to keep every Bible I've ever used. One was destroyed by mildew in storage, but I have all the others. If you examined all those Bibles, you would notice that the pages in the back where the Epistles are found are worn much more than the rest.

Don't misunderstand me. I read and teach the entire Bible — from cover to cover. But many years ago I discovered that the Epistles (or letters from the Apostles) spoke to me in a direct and pointed way. They were written to Christians —

and that includes *me*! So I decided to live in and by the Epistles.

The Old Testament was all the Bible there was for centuries. It was the Bible Jesus quoted from in His ministry. The Old Testament is valuable to me because it teaches me about God, the early history of the world, and how God dealt with His chosen people, the Jews. It contains the Law and the Prophets, the Psalms and Proverbs. I appreciate the Old Testament and benefit from it, but it was not written *to* me.

The four Gospels are tremendous, recording the ministry and teachings of Jesus. By reading the Gospel accounts, I know about the birth of our Lord, His travels, His miracles, His teachings, His prayers, His death and resurrection. The Gospels present the plan of salvation and Christ's Great Commission to evangelize the world. I love the Gospels, but they were written *for* me, not *to* me.

The Acts of the Apostles is a detailed history of the Early Church. It talks about the first believers receiving the baptism in the Holy Spirit on the Day of Pentecost and how churches were established throughout the known world. But again, Acts was written *for* me, not *to* me.

But when I read the Epistles, I find that they are letters written to the Church — to people who are born-again believers, trying to live their daily lives according to the teachings of the

Lord. These letters provide specific teachings I need to understand — guidance, direction, and correction I can use in my own situations.

Many times as I read them I get the feeling that the author, moved upon by the inspiration of the Holy Ghost, looked down through the centuries and saw me struggling to find my way and said, "Go this direction! Follow this example."

Just to be sure we understand that the Epistles are addressed to us, several of the Apostles emphasized that they were writing to a wider audience than the original addressees. For example, in First Corinthians 1:2, Paul addressed a letter saying, "*Unto the church of God which is at Corinth, to them that are sanctified in Christ Jesus, called to be saints, WITH ALL THAT IN EVERY PLACE CALL UPON THE NAME OF JESUS CHRIST OUR LORD. . . .*" That "all in every place" includes you and me.

In his letter "to the saints at Ephesus," Paul also included, "*. . . and to the faithful in Christ Jesus*" (Eph. 1:1). Thank God, I'm trying to be faithful, aren't you? So this letter is written to me.

The Apostle James addressed his letter, "*. . . to the twelve tribes which are scattered abroad . . .*" (James 1:1).

And Peter addressed one of his letters ". . . *to them that have obtained like precious faith with us through the righteousness of God and our Saviour Jesus Christ*" (2 Peter 1:1).

So to me, the Epistles are a little bit extra special. I feel as though their teaching has great relevance to us today who are members of the Body of Christ. I've always found the teaching of the Epistles to be right to the point, clear, and unmistakable.

In this chapter, I have included twenty-four principles from the Epistles that relate to our general topic of money, giving, and prosperity. What the Apostles have to say is so plain that it requires very little commentary, so most of the text that follows is Scripture. And sometimes I compare two or more versions or translations of the same passage.

1. Believers are not able to give anything to God that did not originate with God.

O the depth of the riches both of the wisdom and knowledge of God! how unsearchable are his judgments, and his ways past finding out! For who hath known the mind of the Lord? or who hath been his counsellor? Or who hath first given to him, and it shall be recompensed unto him again?

— Romans 11:33-35

Montgomery's translation of verse 35 says, "Who has first given to Him, So as to receive payment in return?"

This makes it clear that we are not to demand that God give us what we want. God in His graciousness has already provided everything for us.

The Old Testament tells how David wanted to see a house, or temple, built for God and how he collected a generous offering from his personal wealth and from the prosperity of the people of Israel. They amassed an enormous amount of gold, silver, precious stones, and other materials needed for the task. Then David prayed this eloquent prayer:

Thine, O Lord, is the greatness, and the power, and the glory, and the victory, and the majesty: FOR ALL THAT IS IN THE HEAVEN AND IN THE EARTH IS THINE; thine is the kingdom, O Lord, and thou art exalted as head above all. Both riches and honour come of thee, and thou reignest over all; and in thine hand is power and might; and in thine hand it is to make great, and to give strength unto all. Now therefore, our God, we thank thee, and praise thy glorious name. But who am I, and what is my people, that we should be able to offer so willingly after this sort? FOR ALL THINGS COME OF THEE, AND OF THINE OWN HAVE WE GIVEN THEE. . . . O LORD OUR GOD, ALL THIS STORE THAT WE HAVE PREPARED TO BUILD THEE AN HOUSE FOR THINE HOLY NAME COMETH OF THINE OWN HAND, AND IS ALL THINE OWN.

— 1 Chronicles 29:11-14,16

Remember, too, that in First Corinthians 10:26 and 28, Paul declares that the "earth is the Lord's and the fulness thereof."

Both the Old and New Testaments recognize God as the Creator and Possessor of all things. Having given God something does not entitle one to arrogantly demand that God do something in return. Rather, giving is to be done worshipfully, recognizing that whatever we give to God was originally *created* by Him and then *given* to us. Therefore, the proper attitude for giving is one of worship and gratitude.

2. Some believers operate in a special grace of giving.

Having then gifts differing according to the grace that is given to us, whether prophecy, let us prophesy according to the proportion of faith; Or ministry, let us wait on our ministering: or he that teacheth, on teaching; Or he that exhorteth, on exhortation: HE THAT GIVETH, let him do it with simplicity; he that ruleth, with diligence; he that showeth mercy, with cheerfulness.

— Romans 12:6-8

These are not ministerial offices like those listed in Ephesians chapter 4. Rather, they are simply special inclinations found in certain believers based on "extra grace" in a given area. For example, all believers are called upon by God to be merciful, but some have an extra grace in this area.

Some believers are given special grace and abound especially in the area of giving. But this does not excuse other believers from their basic responsibility of giving.

3. Believers are called upon to be diligent in business.

Not slothful in business; fervent in spirit; serving the Lord.

— Romans 12:11

Montgomery's translation of this verse reads, "In your diligence be free from sloth. . . ."

While the Apostle Paul touches on this important topic, the Book of Proverbs is full of admonitions that apply to every believer. Believers cannot expect to prosper if they are not diligent and responsible in discharging their duties in life.

4. Believers are called upon to be responsible toward their financial obligations.

For for this cause pay ye tribute also: for they are God's ministers, attending continually upon this very thing. Render therefore to all their dues: tribute to whom tribute is due; custom to whom custom; fear to whom fear; honour to whom honour. OWE NO MAN ANY THING, BUT TO LOVE ONE ANOTHER: FOR HE THAT LOVETH ANOTHER HATH FULFILLED THE LAW.

— Romans 13:6-8

Weymouth's translation of verse 8 says, "Leave no debt unpaid except the standing debt of mutual love."

5. Believers have a duty to minister financially to those who have spiritually blessed them.

But now I go unto Jerusalem to minister unto the saints.
For it hath pleased them of Macedonia and Achaia to make
a certain contribution for the poor saints which are at
Jerusalem. It hath pleased them verily; and their debtors
they are. For if the Gentiles have been made partakers of
their spiritual things, their duty is also to minister unto them
in carnal things.

— Romans 15:25-27

Let him that is taught in the word communicate unto him
that teacheth in all good things.

— Galatians 6:6

The Phillips translation of Galatians 6:6 says, "The man under Christian instruction should be willing to contribute toward the livelihood of his teacher."

6. Ministers have a right to be supported financially by their work in the ministry.

Have we not power [the right] to eat and to drink? Have
we not power [the right] to lead about a sister, a wife, as
well as other apostles, and as the brethren of the Lord, and

Cephas? Or I only and Barnabas, have not we power [the right] *to forbear working? Who goeth a warfare any time at his own charges? who planteth a vineyard, and eateth not of the fruit thereof? or who feedeth a flock, and eateth not of the milk of the flock? Say I these things as a man? or saith not the law the same also? For it is written in the law of Moses, Thou shalt not muzzle the mouth of the ox that treadeth out the corn. Doth God take care for oxen? Or saith he it altogether for our sakes? For our sakes, no doubt, this is written: that he that ploweth should plow in hope; and that he that thresheth in hope should be partaker of his hope. If we have sown unto you spiritual things, is it a great thing if we shall reap your carnal things?* [The Williams version of this verse says, "If we have sown the spiritual seed for you, is it too great for us to reap a material support from you?"] *If others be partakers of this power* [right] *over you, are not we rather? Nevertheless we have not used this power* [right]*; but suffer all things, lest we should hinder the gospel of Christ. Do ye not know that they which minister about holy things live of the things of the temple? and they which wait at the altar are partakers with the altar? Even so hath the Lord ordained that they which preach the gospel should live of the gospel. But I have used none of these things: neither have I written these things,* *that it should be done unto me: for it were better for me to*

die, than that any man should make my glorying void.

— 1 Corinthians 9:4-15

Notice that Paul stresses that ministers have the right to be supported financially. Even though in one particular circumstance Paul chose to *forfeit* this right rather than be accused of *abusing* that right, he makes a point that he and other ministers deserve to be supported.

Let the elders that rule well be counted worthy of double

honour, especially they who labour in the word and doc-

trine. For the scripture saith, Thou shalt not muzzle the

ox that treadeth out the corn. And, The labourer is wor-

thy of his reward.

— 1 Timothy 5:17,18

The Williams version of verse 17 says, "Elders who do their duties well should be considered as deserving twice the salary they get, especially those who keep on toiling in preaching and teaching."

7. Love must motivate the believer's giving.

And though I bestow all my goods to feed the poor, and

though I give my body to be burned, and have not charity,

it profiteth me nothing.

— 1 Corinthians 13:3

The Modern Language translation says, "And though I give all my belongings to feed the hungry and surrender my body to be burned, but I have no love, I am not in the least benefited."

8. Christians should practice consistent and systematic giving.

Now concerning the collection for the saints, as I have given order to the churches of Galatia, even so do ye. Upon the first day of the week let every one of you lay by him in store, as God has prospered him, that there be no gatherings when I come.

— 1 Corinthians 16:1,2

Verse 2, according to the Norlie translation, stresses that each person's giving should be ". . . according to his financial ability."

The Living Bible says "The amount depends on how much the Lord has helped you earn."

9. Giving is a "grace" that can be exercised in the midst of challenging circumstances. Giving is reflective of a life given to God and is rooted in the Person and example of the Lord Jesus Christ.

Moreover, brethren, we do you to wit of the grace of God bestowed on the churches of Macedonia; How that in a great trial of affliction the abundance of their joy and their deep poverty abounded unto the riches of their liberality. For to their power, I bear record, yea, and beyond their power they were willing of themselves; Praying us with much entreaty that we would receive the gift, and take upon us the fellowship of the ministering to the saints. And this they did, not as we hoped, but first gave their own selves to the Lord, and unto us by the will of God. Insomuch that we desired Titus, that as he had begun, so he would also finish in you the same grace also. Therefore, as ye abound in every thing, in faith, and utterance, and knowledge, and in all diligence, and in your love to us, see that ye abound in this grace also. I speak not by commandment, but by occasion of the forwardness of others, and to prove the sincerity of your love. For ye know the grace of our Lord Jesus Christ, that, though he was rich, yet for your sakes he became poor, that ye through his poverty might be rich.

— 2 Corinthians 8:1-9

Verse 2 in *The New English Bible* reads, "The troubles they have been through have tried them hard, yet in all this they have been so exuberantly happy that from the depths of their poverty they have shown themselves lavishly open-handed."

10. God wants all of us to do our part and to "carry our weight" in giving.

But by an equality, that now at this time your abundance may be a supply for their want, that their abundance also may be a supply for your want: that there may be equality: As it is written, He that had gathered much had nothing over; and he that had gathered little had no lack.

— 2 Corinthians 8:14,15

In this passage, Paul is specifically addressing the issue of prosperous Christians helping struggling Christians, but the concept of equality has other applications also. God wants everyone in the Church to do his or her part. Unfortunately, in many churches, a faithful few carry the financial load while others (who are able to give) are freeloaders. Because of different income levels, people might give *different amounts*, but God wants members of the church to have *equal commitment*.

11. Ministers should be ethical and above reproach in their handling of church finances.

Avoiding this, that no man should blame us in this abundance which is administered by us: Providing for honest things, not only in the sight of the Lord, but also in the sight of men.

— 2 Corinthians 8:20,21

In *The New English Bible*, verse 20 says, "We want to guard against any criticism of our handling of this generous gift." And in the *New International Version*, verse 21 reads, "For we are taking pains to do what is right, not only in the eyes of the Lord but also in the eyes of men."

12. Paul clearly teaches the law of sowing and reaping.

But this I say, He which soweth sparingly shall reap also sparingly; and he which soweth bountifully shall reap also bountifully. Every man according as he purposeth in his heart, so let him give; not grudgingly [sorrowfully], or of necessity [under compulsion]: for God loveth a cheerful giver. And God is able to make all grace abound toward you; that ye, always having all sufficiency in all things, may abound to every good work.

— 2 Corinthians 9:6-8

In *The Twentieth Century New Testament*, verse 8 says, "God has power to shower all kinds of blessings upon you, so that, having, under all circumstances and on all occasions, all that you can need, you may be able to shower all kinds of benefits upon others."

There are other scriptures that teach this law of sowing and reaping.

Be not deceived; God is not mocked: for whatsoever a man soweth, that shall he also reap. For he that soweth to his flesh shall of the flesh reap corruption; but he that soweth to the Spirit shall of the Spirit reap life everlasting. And let us not be weary in well doing: for in due season we shall reap, if we faint not.

— Galatians 6:7-9

Notwithstanding ye have well done, that ye did communicate with my affliction. Now ye Philippians know also, that in the beginning of the gospel, when I departed from Macedonia, no church communicated with me as concerning GIVING AND RECEIVING, but ye only. For even in Thessalonica ye sent once and again unto my necessity. Not because I desire a gift: but I desire fruit that may abound to your account. But I have all, and abound: I am full, having received of Epaphroditus the things which were sent from you, an odour of a sweet smell, a sacrifice acceptable, wellpleasing to God. But my God shall supply all your need according to his riches in glory by Christ Jesus.

— Philippians 4:14-19

13. Paul sought people's *hearts,* not their *money.*

Behold, the third time I am ready to come to you; and I will not be burdensome to you: FOR I SEEK NOT

YOURS, BUT YOU: *for the children ought not to lay up for the parents, but the parents for the children. And I will very gladly spend and be spent for you; though the more abundantly I love you, the less I be loved. But be it so, I did not burden you: nevertheless, being crafty, I caught you with guile. Did I make a gain of you by any of them whom I sent unto you? I desired Titus, and with him I sent a brother. Did Titus make a gain of you? walked we not in the same spirit? walked we not in the same steps?*

— 2 Corinthians 12:14-18

14. Paul was eager to give to the poor.

And when James, Cephas, and John, who seemed to be pillars, perceived the grace that was given unto me, they gave to me and Barnabas the right hands of fellowship; that we should go unto the heathen, and they unto the circumcision. Only they would that we should remember the poor; the same which I also was forward [eager] to do.

— Galatians 2:9,10

15. Paul and John encouraged Christian charity among the brethren.

As we have therefore opportunity, let us do good unto all men, especially unto them who are of the household of faith.

— Galatians 6:10

But whoso hath this world's good, and seeth his brother have need, and shutteth up his bowels of compassion from him, how dwelleth the love of God in him? My little children, let us not love in word, neither in tongue; but in deed and in truth.

— 1 John 3:17,18

16. Paul exemplified and taught a strong work ethic.

Let him that stole steal no more: but rather let him labour, working with his hands the thing which is good, that he may have to give to him that needeth.

— Ephesians 4:28

Servants, be obedient to them that are your masters according to the flesh, with fear and trembling, in singleness of your heart, as unto Christ; Not with eyeservice, as menpleasers; but as the servants of Christ, doing the will of God from the heart; With good will doing service, as to the Lord, and not to men: Knowing that whatsoever good thing any man doeth, the same shall he receive of the Lord, whether he be bond or free.

— Ephesians 6:5-8

Servants, obey in all things your masters according to the flesh; not with eyeservice as menpleasers; but in singleness of heart, fearing God: And whatsoever ye do, do it heartily, as to the Lord, and not unto men; Knowing that of the Lord ye shall receive the reward of the inheritance: for ye serve the Lord Christ.

— Colossians 3:22-24

For ye remember, brethren, our labour and travail: for labouring night and day, because we would not be chargeable unto any of you, we preached unto you the gospel of God.

— 1 Thessalonians 2:9

. . . study to be quiet, and to do your own business, and to work with your hands, as we commanded you; That ye may walk honestly toward them that are without, and that ye may have lack of nothing.

— 1 Thessalonians 4:11,12

Neither did we eat any man's bread for nought; but wrought with labour and travail night and day, that we might not be chargeable to any of you: Not because we have not power [the right], but to make ourselves an ensample unto you to follow us. For even when we were with you, this we commanded you, that IF ANY WOULD NOT WORK, NEITHER SHOULD HE EAT. For we hear that there are some which walk among you disorderly, working not at all, but are busy-bodies. Now them that are such we command and exhort

*by our Lord Jesus Christ, that with quietness they work,
and eat their own bread.*

— 2 Thessalonians 3:8-12

17. Paul advocated contentment and denounced covetousness.

*Not that I speak in respect of want: for I have learned,
in whatsoever state I am, therewith to be content. I
know both how to be abased, and I know how to
abound: every where and in all things I am instructed
both to be full and to be hungry, both to abound and to
suffer need. I can do all things through Christ which
strengtheneth me.*

— Philippians 4:11-13

*Let your conversation be without covetousness; and be
content with such things as ye have: for he hath said, I
will never leave thee, nor forsake thee.*

— Hebrews 13:5

*This is a true saying, If a man desire the office of a bishop,
he desireth a good work. A bishop then must be blameless,
the husband of one wife, vigilant, sober, of good behaviour,
given to hospitality, apt to teach; Not given to wine, no
striker, not greedy of filthy lucre; but patient, not a
brawler, not covetous. . . . Likewise must the deacons be*

grave, not doubletongued, not given to much wine, not
greedy of filthy lucre.

— 1 Timothy 3:1-3,8

For a bishop must be blameless, as the steward of God;
not selfwilled, not soon angry, not given to wine, no
striker, not given to filthy lucre.

— Titus 1:7

The lie of covetousness is: "If only I had more money," or
"If only I had such and such, I would be happy." But contentment says, "Because of Jesus Christ, I am happy no matter
what the circumstances."

18. Paul stressed the individual's responsibility to provide for his family.

But if any provide not for his own, and specially for those
of his own house, he hath denied the faith, and is worse
than an infidel.

— 1 Timothy 5:8

19. Believers are not to love or trust in money.

Perverse disputings of men of corrupt minds, and destitute
of the truth, supposing that gain is godliness: from such
withdraw thyself. But godliness with contentment is great
gain. For we brought nothing into this world, and it is cer-
tain we can carry nothing out. And having food and rai-

ment let us be therewith content. But they that will be rich

fall into temptation and a snare, and into many foolish and

hurtful lusts, which drown men in destruction and perdi-

tion. For the love of money is the root of all evil: which

while some coveted after, they have erred from the faith,

and pierced themselves through with many sorrows. . . .

Charge them that are rich in this world, that they be not

highminded, nor trust in uncertain riches, but in the living

God, who giveth us richly all things to enjoy; That they do

good, that they be rich in good works, ready to distribute,

willing to communicate; Laying up in store for themselves

a good foundation against the time to come, that they may

lay hold on eternal life.

— 1 Timothy 6:5-10,17-19

20. Believers in the Early Church considered their material possessions of much less value than their faith.

But call to remembrance the former days, in which, after

ye were illuminated, ye endured a great fight of afflic-

tions; Partly, whilst ye were made a gazingstock both by

reproaches and afflictions; and partly, whilst ye became

companions of them that were so used. For ye had com-

passion of me in my bonds, and took joyfully the spoiling

*of your goods, knowing in yourselves that ye have in
heaven a better and an enduring substance.*

— Hebrews 10:32-34

The Williams translation of verse 34 says, ". . . and cheerfully submitted to the violent seizure of your property, for you knew
that you had in yourselves and in heaven one that was lasting."

21. Believers were strongly warned against favoritism and partiality based on wealth.

*My brethren, have not the faith of our Lord Jesus Christ,
the Lord of glory, with respect of persons. For if there
come unto your assembly a man with a gold ring, in
goodly apparel, and there come in also a poor man in vile
raiment; And ye have respect to him that weareth the
gay clothing, and say unto him, Sit thou here in a good
place; and say to the poor, Stand thou there, or sit here
under my footstool: Are ye not then partial in yourselves, and are become judges of evil thoughts? Hearken,
my beloved brethren, Hath not God chosen the poor of
this world rich in faith, and heirs of the kingdom which
he hath promised to them that love him? But ye have
despised the poor. Do not rich men oppress you, and
draw you before the judgment seats? Do not they blas-
pheme that worthy name by the which ye are called?*

— James 2:1-7

22. Exploitation of the poor by the rich is condemned.

Go to now, ye rich men, weep and howl for your miseries that shall come upon you. Your riches are corrupted, and your garments are motheaten. Your gold and silver is cankered; and the rust of them shall be a witness against you, and shall eat your flesh as it were fire. Ye have heaped treasure together for the last days. Behold, the hire of the labourers who have reaped down your fields, which is of you kept back by fraud, crieth: and the cries of them which have reaped are entered into the ears of the Lord of Sabaoth. Ye have lived in pleasure on the earth, and been wanton; ye have nourished your hearts, as in a day of slaughter. Ye have condemned and killed the just; and he doth not resist you.

— James 5:1-6

23. "Making merchandise" of the saints by ministers is condemned.

And many shall follow their pernicious [highly injurious or destructive] *ways; by reason of whom the way of truth shall be evil spoken of. And through covetousness shall they with feigned* [not genuine] *words make merchandise of you: whose judgment now of a long time lingereth not, and their damnation slumbereth not.*

— 2 Peter 2:2,3

The Phillips translation of verse 2 says, "Many will follow their pernicious teaching and thereby bring discredit on the way of truth."

Notice some other translations of verse 3:

"Motivated by greed, they will exploit you with their counterfeit arguments" (*Modern Language*).

"In their covetousness they will try to make you a source of profit by their fabrications" (*The Twentieth Century New Testament*).

"In their greed they will exploit you with messages manufactured by themselves" (*Williams*).

"These teachers in their greed will tell you anything to get hold of your money" (*TLB*).

Second Peter chapter 2 records another passage regarding this issue.

> *But these, as natural brute beasts, made to be taken and destroyed, speak evil of the things that they understand not; and shall utterly perish in their own corruption; And shall receive the reward of unrighteousness, as they that count it pleasure to riot in the day time. Spots they are and blemishes, sporting themselves with their own deceivings while they feast with you; Having eyes full of adultery, and that cannot cease from sin; beguiling unstable souls: an heart they have exercised with covetous practices;*

cursed children: Which have forsaken the right way, and
are gone astray, following the way of Balaam the son of
Bosor, who loved the wages of unrighteousness; But was
rebuked for his iniquity: the dumb ass speaking with man's
voice forbad the madness of the prophet.

— 2 Peter 2:12-16

24. God wants His children to prosper.

Beloved, I wish above all things that thou mayest prosper
and be in health, even as thy soul prospereth.

— 3 John 2

Weymouth's translation of this verse says, "Dearly loved one, I pray that you may in all respects prosper and keep well."

The Twentieth Century New Testament says, "Dear friend, I pray that all may be well with you and that you may have good health."

As I mentioned in Chapter 1 of this book, some people have argued that the phrase "that thou mayest prosper" does not refer to *financial* prosperity. According to both Wuest's *Word Studies in the New Testament* and Robertson's *Word Pictures in the New Testament*, the Greek word translated "prospereth" is "euodoo," which means *a good road* or *a good journey.* So at the very least, the phrase meant to have a good and prosperous journey.

No one can have a good and prosperous journey if he is broke, lacking, in poverty, and in want every step of the way. Wouldn't the wish for someone to have a prosperous journey include his having enough resources to travel safely and comfortably?

Besides, the word translated "prosper" here is the same Greek word Paul used in First Corinthians 16:2 where he instructed the believers to set aside some money each week "as God hath *prospered* him." So the word prosper can certainly and without doubt be used — and is used — in reference to financial prosperity.

I believe this verse clearly means that God wants His children to prosper materially, physically, and spiritually.

I pray these Bible principles selected from the Epistles will be helpful and encouraging to you. I urge you to study them carefully and refer to them often. Remember, the Epistles were written to *you*!

CHAPTER NINE

WALKING IN THE LIGHT

In this book, I've shared some of the lessons I've learned concerning biblical prosperity during my years of ministry. I've tried to present a sound, practical, balanced approach to this important subject, basing everything I've said on the solid foundation of the Word of God.

My purpose in writing this book is to provide a clear statement of the scriptural truths of prosperity — truths I believe with all my heart. By stating in a spirit of love what the Bible says is right and true, I hope to help all believers claim the precious promises of God and avoid the ditches of error, extremism, and confusion that lie on both sides of the road.

Early on in my ministry, I struggled against the limitations of poverty and lack until I learned that God indeed wanted me to "eat the good of the land" (Isa. 1:19). I discovered that God's promise was for me to thrive and flourish in every aspect of my being — spiritually, physically, materially, *and* financially.

In an attempt to clarify and cast light on an area of misunderstanding, we examined in depth the question about whether Jesus' earthly life was one of poverty or prosperity. In Chapter 2, we looked at ten compelling scriptural facts that prove Jesus did not live in privation and defeat. He lived a prosperous life in that He always had the resources necessary to do God's work and fulfill God's will.

We also spent an entire chapter studying the vitally important issue of the purpose of prosperity. Every believer has been charged with the responsibility of helping to carry out the Great Commission — of preaching the Gospel in all the world and to every creature. We must either go ourselves or help send someone in our place. Either way requires significant resources. But *going* or *sending* is the true purpose of prosperity.

God's plan for His people includes ways to empower and equip them to do His work and live in victory. We took a look at the law of sowing and reaping, timeless truths about tithing, and numerous good and valid reasons for giving. These are life-changing, transforming principles for success and victory in life.

We examined the crucial issue of providing proper support for the local church, individual ministers and ministries, and the responsibilities of men and women of God in seeking support. All these issues are dealt with forthrightly in God's Word — the information is readily available to those who honestly want the Lord's guidance.

In Chapter 5, I dealt with several specific problems and concerns that have caused confusion and misunderstandings in the Body of Christ. My approach is not to accuse or attack anyone. Many times I've found that those who are off in the ditch on one side of the road or the other are not necessarily bad people. Often they get off track when their zeal exceeds their wisdom.

However, in this book I have addressed abuses and false practices that clearly violate the definite, specific teachings of the Bible. The Word of God is clear. And the only answer for error is truth. Jesus said, "*And ye shall know the truth, and the truth shall make you free*" (John 8:32).

Throughout this book, I have tried to stress balance and sound teaching, presenting the whole counsel of God. In addition to my own discoveries and studies, I have presented the wisdom and experience of some great men of God whom I have admired and respected over the years.

An extremely important section of the book is Chapter 7, which presents twenty-four principles from the Epistles regarding money, giving, and prosperity. You'll want to read and study these scriptural principles over and over again. I think they should be marked in your own Bible, and you may also want to memorize many of these verses.

But most important of all, the best thing I can do for you in this book is to point you to Jesus. If you are still struggling with doubts or misunderstandings, if you feel you have gone astray into a ditch on the side of the road, or if you need further direction and guidance — Jesus is your answer! He said, *"I am the light of the world: he that followeth me shall not walk in darkness, but shall have the light of life"* (John 8:12).

God wants you to have all the information and knowledge you need to walk in victory and power. And He said in His Word, *"Call unto me, and I will answer thee, and shew thee great and mighty things, which thou knowest not"* (Jer. 33:3).

I encourage you to call on the Lord today. Let Him give you knowledge and understanding concerning His Word. Walking in the light of God's Word is what will keep you balanced in the area of prosperity and in *every* area of life.